# MIRIAM

# MIRIAM

*Iris Rosofsky*

COLLINS

*To my editor, Charlotte Zolotow,*
*who showed me that when*
*some doors close, new ones open*

William Collins Sons & Co Ltd
London · Glasgow · Sydney · Auckland
Toronto · Johannesburg

First published by Harper & Row,
Publishers, New York 1988
First published in Great Britain 1989
Copyright © 1988 Iris Rosofsky

A CIP catalogue record for this book is
available from the British Library.

ISBN 0 00 185243-4

Printed and bound in Great Britain by
Mackays of Chatham PLC, Kent

# PART
# 1

# CHAPTER
# 1

I was four years old, coming with Mama and Papa to see my new baby brother for the first time—wondering how his presence would change things for me. I walked between them down the long, fluorescent-lit corridor listening to the click-clack of our steps and trying not to inhale the cool antiseptic smell I associated with visits to the doctor's office. When we reached the nursery and a lady in white brought a tiny, wrinkled baby for us to see through the window, I started to cry. I wanted my brother to be something wonderful and special— but instead he resembled a shriveled white raisin. I thought the other babies were all nicer. When I asked Mama if we could have one of the others instead, she laughed and said, "No, mommele. God gave us this one to love. Just like He gave us you."

When we came home, all Mama and Papa talked about was "making everything ready for the baby" and "when will the briss be."

"What's a briss?" I asked.

"It's a party for a Jewish baby when he's eight days old. It's when he becomes one of the Jewish people.

But your brother was too tiny and too sick to have it, so we have to wait till he gets stronger."

"Did I have a briss?"

Mama smiled. "Only boy babies have a briss."

I had wondered what Mama meant by "when he becomes one of the Jewish people." She had said that all Jewish people made blessings, and I made blessings. But I didn't have a briss. Would my brother be more Jewish than I? Would God love him more than me? Did Mama and Papa love him more?

The crib now stood in Mama and Papa's room right between their beds. It was still my crib, even though I was sleeping in a real bed.

One day, they said, "We're bringing your brother home tomorrow. Aren't you happy?" I said, "Yes," but I wasn't so sure. The next day they took me to Tante's and they went to the hospital in a taxi and brought him home. Tante Sophie and Cousin Rosie and Uncle Yitzrok and I came upstairs to see him. But he was wrapped in a blue blanket so you couldn't see anything. They put him in my crib without even asking me.

All week, we got ready for the briss. Papa came home in the middle of the day with packages from the store. He stayed only a minute, just long enough to give Mama all the things he brought, but it made it seem like a holiday to see Papa home when he was usually in the store. He took cheeses out of his pockets. I had never seen cheeses that were round like these and wrapped in pretty red cellophane. And he brought brown paper bags that smelled of herring, and boxes of cookies, and packages of pretty blue paper cups and plates. Every day he brought more. One day, he removed a small white bag from inside his coat and gave it to me. Inside were long, skinny pieces of orange peel all covered with sweet chocolate. Mama said, "Peretz, it's not good for her," but Papa laughed and said, "Just this once, Sarah. It won't hurt her. It's a mitzvah to be happy."

And Mama said, "We have enough already. It's not such a mitzvah to take more than we need."

Then Papa's voice got loud, and his face became red. "What do you mean, 'take'?" he said. "We're partners. Don't you think he takes plenty from me when he's always staying home to take care of his mother so I have to work twice as hard? That's 'taking,' too, isn't it?"

And Mama said, "You don't have to shout, Peretz. I'm not deaf." Her voice was very soft, so I could hardly hear what she was saying, only I saw how her lips moved, so I knew. The softer she spoke, the louder Papa spoke, till the difference between them became very great; it all happened so quickly. I became scared, because I didn't understand; it seemed to me I must have done something wrong, and I wanted to give back the candy.

"No, you eat it, mommele. It's for you," Papa said. And he pushed it back at me when I held it out. But he looked at Mama while he spoke as though he were really saying it to her. I felt as though I shouldn't be taking it because it was causing so much trouble. I looked at Mama to see what she wanted me to do, but she was looking at Papa.

"I only don't want you should turn a mitzvah into a sin." And again she was only whispering, so I could hardly hear.

"I don't understand you, Sarah, I really don't." Papa stopped shouting, but his tone was bitter and cutting. I felt frightened, and I started to cry, but then I stopped myself, because I wanted Mama to hold me, and I wanted Papa to pat me on the head, only not the way they were now, because they were different; they didn't seem like Mama and Papa at all.

"If you don't want a nice briss, a briss everyone will talk about, a briss I can afford to give my son, then don't talk to me about what your brother-in-law gives to your sister, you hear me? You married me! This is what I can afford! I'm sorry it's not good enough!"

Then Mama covered her face with her hands. "Oh, Peretz, I didn't mean that! You know I didn't. I'm sorry—"

"I'm never good enough," he said.

And Mama shook her head and said, "I didn't mean it that way. I didn't mean that." And then neither one of them said anything, but Papa kept staring at her. When she took her hands away, her face was all wet. I wanted to put my arms around her like she did to me whenever I cried, only I was still afraid.

"I'm sorry, Peretz. I'm—overtired," she said. And he went to her and put his arms around her the way I wanted to do, and he said, "I know you are, Sarah. It's hard." And I wanted them to hold me, too. I didn't want to be left out. But I was glad they were making up.

6

So I went into the baby's room to see if he was frightened, but he was sleeping as he always slept, and he didn't even know I was there.

After that, whenever Mama and Papa got angry and I felt frightened, I went into the baby's room, because he was always resting so quietly and he never got scared, and that made me feel peaceful too. Sometimes I put my hand through the bars of the crib and let it rest on top of the blankets where his back was or his belly, to feel how it moved—up–down, up–down, so softly as he breathed. I almost didn't mind him being so small; he was nice that way. I thought he would be all cuddly if Mama would let me hold him. But most of the time she didn't even let me close because of the germs.

# CHAPTER
# 2

The day of the briss was sunny and cold. The sky was like blue glass. Mama kept saying, "I hope people don't stay away because of the cold."

And Papa said, "Don't worry. We have enough schnapps and herring to warm an army."

And he spread out all the things he had brought from the store—the shiny herring on one plate and three more plates with the cheeses. He gave me the red cellophanes so I could hold them against the window and see the world magically endowed in rubies and garnets. Everything looked wonderful to me that way, even the chimney pipes and the bricks and the big clangy garbage cans down below. Only, when I took away the cellophane, then the world looked gray and dull and very ordinary. I had a whole collection of cellophanes—reds and oranges and blues and yellows and greens from lollipops and presents and Purim baskets of candy and fruit. I kept the cellophanes in my toy box, and whenever I was feeling lonely or bored, I took them out and pressed them to the window one by one.

Mama came out of the bedroom dressed in her blue holiday dress, with her hair pinned up like a crown, as she sometimes wore it on the Sabbath, Shabbos. To me, she looked like a queen.

"Let me dress her now," she said to Papa, and she took me by the hand and we walked to my room. I knew something special was going to happen, because Mama held my hand only in the street. She smiled and said, "Now close your eyes!" so I did.

"Ready?" she said. And her voice went up at the end like a cat's tail. "Open!"

There on my bed was the most beautiful dress I had ever seen. It was pink with shiny pockets, and it had a puffy slip that made it stand out as though the wind were blowing.

"Do you like it?" Mama asked, but she was laughing because she knew I loved it. I threw my arms around her, and she laughed some more and said, "This was once my dress when I was a flower girl at your Great-Tante Emma's wedding."

I didn't know what a flower girl was or who Great-Tante Emma was, but it didn't matter. It was Mama's dress, and now she was giving it to me, so she knew I wasn't a baby anymore. I decided a flower girl must be a wonderful thing to be, like a princess or a queen.

"Hold your arms up," Mama said. And she slipped the dress over my head.

"Go show Papa."

I knew Poppy would think I was beautiful.

"That's my little princess!" he said. I wanted him to lift me in the air the way he sometimes did, but he only smiled and repeated, "My little princess."

"I'm Queen Esther!" I told him.

"Queen Esther?" He raised his eyebrows. "That's even better!" But he had stopped smiling, as though Mama and I had disappeared, and he continued to set out the food.

Mama said, "Come on, mommele, there's more." And she held out her hand to me, but I felt she was really talking to Papa. Her face darkened like a rain cloud, but then it grew bright again, and we went back to my room.

"Close your eyes!" she said again, but I peeked, and I saw her take something out of a very small box in her pocket. She came behind me, and I felt her cool hands on the back of my neck in between my curls.

"There!" she said. "Go look in the mirror."

Around my neck was a tiny golden Mogen David, a Star of David.

"This was mine when I was a girl," Mama said. "And it was my mama's before that and her mama's before that. And now it belongs to you."

I felt very important. Someday, I would be a mama too. I was wearing her dress and her Mogen David, and I would grow up to be just like her.

Mama carried the baby into the dining room all wrapped in a new white blanket. Everyone crowded around to get a look. They all went "Ooooooh!" and "Aaaah!" and "Isn't he cute!" and "Ken-eine ha'ra!" You'd think they'd never seen a baby before. I went with Poppy to open the door whenever somebody new came.

"Mazel tov, Peretz! Mazel tov!"

"Such simcha—mazel tov!"

"Is this the sister? Mazel tov, dear! Aren't you happy?"

I was happy we were having a party, but I wished it would start so I could eat the cookies and we could sing. I got tired of people asking me, "Aren't you happy?" or, "Aren't you a lucky little girl to have such a cute brother?" No one noticed my new dress or my Mogen David. I wished Cousin Rosie and Tante Sophie would come.

Then the doorbell rang again; the new guest was so tall that Papa suddenly looked like a little boy next to him. I was surprised and frightened to see Poppy look so small. But Poppy didn't seem to mind. He shook the man's hand and said, "Come in, come in!" And the man said, "Thank you. Mazel tov!" Then Poppy called out, "The moel is here!" and people said, "Aah—the moel!" and, "He's here. We can start!" I didn't know what a moel was. I thought it must be someone very big, but I was glad he came, because someone said, "Now we can start," and I wanted a cookie.

Poppy took the man into their bedroom, and then everyone continued talking again as though they forgot the party was about to begin.

"When are Cousin Rosie and Tante Sophie coming?" I asked Mama. She gave me a funny look, sort of a smile, only her mouth turned down instead of up at the corners.

"That's who we're waiting for now," she said. "Count on my sister to be late!" I thought I must have said something wrong, because Mama suddenly seemed angry. But then she smiled at me and said, "Soon. They'll be here soon, mommele."

Then the moel emerged from the bedroom in a long white robe and a white yarmulke that sat high on his head like a crown. Everyone stood up. Papa took the baby from Mama and brought him to the man and, again, Poppy seemed like a little boy, and I didn't like it. The moel said something to Poppy and Poppy spoke to Mama, and then Mama said, "We're going to start. The moel has to leave soon. We can't wait for my sister."

I felt bad that Tante and Cousin Rosie were going to miss the party, and I thought I would try to save some cookies for them.

All the women crowded together, whispering and smiling, and they hurried out of the room while the men all walked to one side near the big chair where Poppy had brought the folding table. Mama took me by the hand.

"What are they going to do to the baby?" I asked.

"The moel has to make a tiny cut in the baby's skin— to fulfill a covenant our father Abraham made with God."

"What's a cov—a cov—"

"A covenant is an agreement."

"Why did—?"

"Shhh, mommele. Don't ask so many questions." And she pushed me into the huddle of ladies all smelling from perfume and powder, which I liked, only it was so strong it was hard to breathe; all I could see were the ladies' skirts and their pocketbooks and their shoes. I thought that grown-up parties were certainly very strange, but they all seemed to be having a good time talking and laughing.

Then it got very quiet, and I heard Papa say something in Hebrew, and then the moel said something, and then it became quiet again.

Mama put her arms around me and pressed me very close. Suddenly the baby screamed and cried louder than I had ever heard him. I didn't know so much noise could be inside such a tiny baby. Mama's fingers dug into my shoulders. A few of the ladies took deep breaths and let it out like a whoooooooosh of air. Someone told Mama, "Don't cry. It's all over." And then everyone began talking at once and saying, "Mazel tov! Mazel tov!" and the ladies went back to the dining room. Mama kneeled down beside me and hugged me and whispered, "Baruch Ha Shem. Baruch Ha Shem." I knew she was thanking God for something, but I didn't know what. Maybe it was because now the party could begin.

Then the doorbell rang again. Tante Sophie and Cousin Rosie had finally come. Tante's face and her eyes were all red, and as soon as she hugged Mama, she started to cry, and the two of them went into the bedroom.

"What's the matter?" I asked Cousin Rosie.

"Papa left again," she said. Her fists were clenched by her side as though she wanted to punch somebody. But instead, she drew in a deep breath and muttered, "He'll be back." I couldn't tell whether that made her happy or angry. I tried to imagine what it would feel like if my poppy went away, but it was too awful to think about. Sometimes, when he was very busy and he had to stay at the store, I went to bed without seeing him, but I always knew he would come home. I didn't want to think about that now, because it made me very sad for Rosie.

"You can hold my dolly," I said to her, and I let her hold it so she would feel better.

When Mama came out of the bedroom with Tante, I could tell she had been crying, too. She didn't notice me standing there, so Rosie and I filled our pockets with cookies and went into my room to play. But I kept thinking.

"Why is Mama crying?" I asked Rosie.

"She always cries when Papa takes off."

"No. I mean, why is my mama crying?"

"I don't know. Ask her."

"Okay." But I knew I wouldn't, though I didn't know why. So I wheeled my doll carriage over to Rosie and we started to play.

# CHAPTER
# 3

Uncle Yitzrok's visits after supper were a regular occurrence. For a long time, I felt frightened of him. I would hide behind Mama or run to my room whenever he sat in our kitchen and invited me to sit on his lap. He would pat his thighs and laugh and say, "Come, mommele, sit here. Be my little girl." But I didn't want to be his little girl. I belonged to Mama and Poppy. His big black beard covered his whole face, so you couldn't see his mouth. Sometimes his tongue, dark pink and shiny, would dart up and down or flit across his lips (or where I knew his lips must be under all that hair), but it wasn't the same as being able to see his mouth when he spoke. I always felt he was hiding something. I used to think it had to do with strange mystical powers. I felt Mama knew his secret, because I sometimes caught her gazing at him as though she were reading his heart, but then she would turn away quickly when she saw me watching her. Uncle Yitzrok always inquired about Moshele and went in to see him, even when he was already asleep in his crib, so I assumed that he would be sharing his secrets with my brother as soon as he was old enough to understand. I've since come to wonder whether it was Moshe's superior intellect or the fact that he was a boy—or was it some other, darker secret?—that drew Uncle and my brother together.

On Sunday, Uncle Yitzrok came especially to see Moshe. They would sit on the sofa together with a big book between them, or sometimes Moshe would sit on his lap. Mama kept me out of the dining room then.

"Don't bother them," she said. "Your brother is learning." I wanted to learn, too. I was already in first grade, but that wasn't the same. Moshe's learning with Uncle Yitzrok seemed more important; it seemed mysterious. When I practiced the alphabet or writing my name or singing the songs I learned in school, no one kept quiet, but when Moshele was learning, we all spoke in whispers and tiptoed around the house.

Sometimes, when I heard them singing in Hebrew, I would stand in the doorway and listen. Uncle would be tapping his feet on the floor, bouncing Moshe up and down in his lap while my brother clapped. Or they would dance in the middle of the room, holding hands and walking in a circle, and sometimes stamping or kicking their feet. It looked like fun, and I wanted to join them, but Mama said I mustn't interrupt.

When Uncle was singing and dancing with Moshe, his beard never frightened me. It made me want to be near him so I could learn the secrets he was sharing with my brother.

Sometimes we wouldn't see Uncle Yitzrok for weeks. Moshe could never understand why Uncle would miss his Sunday morning sessions. I felt sorry for Moshe; he looked so sad then, as though he had lost something precious. Papa would study with him, but it wasn't the same, because Papa never sang or danced. When Uncle Yitzrok wasn't there, I didn't bother listening in the doorway.

Whenever Uncle disappeared, Mama would sigh and tell Papa, "He took off again."

I used to picture him flying out the window high over Brooklyn like an airplane, with his long black frockcoat flapping in the breeze. Rosie used to look very sad when her poppy "took off." I thought she was afraid he would crash and hurt himself. Only when we were older, around eight or nine, did I understand that his taking off meant he had left home for days or weeks at a time. It was information I got from eavesdropping on Mama and Poppy, because Rosie never talked about it anymore, and Mama had warned me, "Never ask about Uncle Yitzrok. You mustn't ask about family matters." From this, I learned that I mustn't discuss our "family matters," either—though I wasn't quite sure what a "family matter" was. Gradually, I learned that it was all right to talk about school and about my health and my brother's health, and even to boast a little—but not too much, for fear of incurring the "evil eye"—about Moshe's rapid progress in learning, but I must never say anything about Mama's or Papa's health, and never, never about "the store" or "the Partner" or about anything I heard them discuss. Mama instructed me, "If anyone asks you questions in shul or on the street, say, 'Everyone's fine, thank God,' or, 'I don't know.' " In this way, I came to feel that we were guarding some very important secret and that someday I would be grown up enough to be trusted with it.

# CHAPTER
## 4

Rosie and I spent a lot of time together after school. Mama always preferred that we play in our house, as long as we didn't disturb Moshe—but she let me go to Rosie's anyway. It was so different there. Tante Sophie was always bustling around the stove or sitting in front of the television. Wherever you went, even in Rosie's room, you could hear the programs.

Uncle Yitzrok wasn't home much. I thought it must be awfully lonely for Rosie to eat supper with just her mother. Who could she talk to if Tante was always watching TV? At our dinner table there was lots of talk, and I looked forward to Shabbos, when Rosie ate with us. Then everything was wonderful.

In Rosie's house we played in her room and closed the door. Then, even with the television noise, we were alone in our own world. It could be anywhere—we played at house and outer space and actresses; we played dominoes and pickup sticks. It didn't matter, as long as it was with Rosie.

"Guess what?" she said one afternoon.

"What?"

"Close your eyes!"

I closed my eyes. I heard her walk to the corner near her bed and open what sounded like a suitcase. Then I heard a high-pitched scraping sound that gave me goose bumps.

"Okay. You can open them."

I did. Rosie stood before me with a violin in one hand and a bow in the other.

"I can play the violin! I'm going to be in the school orchestra. You want me to play something for you?"

"Okay."

"What do you want to hear?"

"I don't know."

"Come on. Pick something."

I thought about it. "Rock of Ages!"

Rosie screwed up her face. "Pick something else."

"Hanukkah, Oh, Hanukkah!"

"Don't you know any good songs?"

"What's wrong with those?"

"Can't you think of anything else besides being Jewish?"

I felt tears come to my eyes, but they didn't come out. I couldn't bear it when Rosie was irritated with me. Of course I knew other songs. I loved the Beatles. I knew all the words to most of their songs from listening to Rosie's albums. But I knew Mama and Papa wouldn't approve of the Beatles, so I didn't feel right about asking Rosie to play them on the violin. A record seemed different, because it wasn't really us making the music.

Rosie's voice softened. "All right. I'll pick something. Sit down."

I sat on her bed and waited. The shrill, scratchy sounds were worse than before.

"It was very pretty," I said. "What's the name of it?"

"It's the 'C major scale.' "

I tried to remember it, should I ever hear it again.

Tante knocked on the door and entered. "I baked a fudge cake," she said, presenting each of us with a thick slice on a plate.

I didn't know what to do. Mama let me come to Rosie's only on condition that I not eat a thing there.

"She doesn't know what kosher is," Mama had warned. "She doesn't follow the dietary laws. Don't take anything from her."

But the cake looked so good. And how could I make Tante feel bad by refusing? But what if Mama found out and forbade me to visit Rosie ever again! I didn't know what to do."

"I have a bellyache," I mumbled. "I better not."

"Bellyache, shmelly-ache. A little piece of cake won't do you any harm. It's good for you."

"No—thank you, Tante. I better not."

"I'll leave it here, anyway," she said. "Rosie, essen. It's good."

"Okay."

Tante left.

Rosie picked at the icing. It looked so chocolaty and sweet I could practically taste it.

When Tante left, Rosie declared, "When I grow up I'm going to be a musician. I'll play the violin all over the world!"

"Why do you have to go all over the world? Can't you just stay here and play?"

"I want to become a music star and be famous. No one becomes famous in Borough Park."

Rosie's plans made me sad. I couldn't bear the idea of Rosie leaving me.

I knew more of Cousin Rosie's and Tante's life than anyone knew I did. I felt very important in front of Mama for not revealing their "family matters" and for not even letting on that I knew. And I felt grown up and trusted by Tante because she never sent me out of the room when they were having one of their heated "family matters." I must have been about eight when I began noticing how different Uncle was in his own house. He never smiled or laughed, and I hardly heard him speak except when he and Tante argued. I didn't like to hear them argue. I would reach for Rosie's hand secretly, and we would squeeze each other's fingers every time Tante and Uncle raised their voices. Rosie's hands were sweaty and cold. We never spoke about these fights afterward, yet I knew that my being there to share what she was feeling was important.

One day, as Uncle Yitzrok was storming out of the house and Rosie and I were standing in the vestibule near the door, Uncle stopped suddenly. He looked Rosie in the eye; his voice softened.

"Would you girls like to go for a walk with me?"

I looked at Rosie to see how I should respond. She didn't return my gaze, but kept staring at her papa. It was as though I had disappeared. When she spoke, I could scarcely hear her.

"Yes, Papa. I'd like to go." The way she emphasized "I'd" left me out completely. I understood that she wanted to be alone with her papa. But I was surprised, since she never talked about him with me. Whenever I brought up his name, she always seemed angry and either kept silent or changed the subject.

They left together and I remained, wondering what to do.

I was just about to leave when Tante called to me from the kitchen. "Miriam, come keep me company."

I sat down across the table from her, though by this time I really wanted to leave, too.

She turned down the television sound.

"Here, mommele, have some cake. You must be hungry." Sitting two feet from Tante, with the cake between us on the table, I found it hard to refuse. The scent of chocolate fudge was all over. I decided it would be less of a sin if, instead of saying okay, I just kept quiet and let her place a slice in front of me. That way, I could eat the nonkosher cake without actually agreeing to eat it.

Tante began telling me things as though I were an adult. "I can't take his moods anymore. He comes in, he goes out. He never tells me where he's going or when he'll be back. You think I know what he does? I don't know what he does."

She reached for my hand on the table and held it tightly.

"Nothing I do is good enough. He expects me to clean up every speck of dust—and make for him big Shabbos dinners. He doesn't talk to me. I can't take it."

Then she was quiet. When I looked at her face, there were two giant tears running down her cheeks and her eyes were all red. She pressed her lips tight and her face became wrinkly.

"But I miss him!" she cried. "I miss him when he's not here. I miss him!"

I felt very uncomfortable. I didn't know what to say. I wanted to defend Uncle Yitzrok, but I felt I should keep quiet.

She rested her head in her hands, covering her face. When she didn't look at me again for a few minutes, I whispered, "I better go now. I have to do my homework."

She nodded consent without looking up.

So I got my coat and left as quietly as I could.

I knew Tante trusted that I would not reveal her secrets.

# CHAPTER
## 5

It was during the next year or so that I began sensing that things were different in all sorts of ways than I'd always thought they were. It seemed to start with our trips to Poppy's store. Mama sometimes took us there when I came home from school. All the customers knew us, and they would stop to pinch Moshe's cheek or ask Mama, "How is he getting on?" I liked to watch Papa behind the counter in his white apron, carefully slicing the lox with his long knife or putting a whole Muenster or Swiss cheese on a shiny metal contraption and then pressing a button and watching it go *zzzzzzzzzzzzzzzzz!* and big slices of yellow cheese, like pages from a book, would drop to the wooden counter. Sometimes, if a piece came out too small or uneven, he would reach over the counter and give it to me. The whole store smelled of garlic pickles, which was how Poppy usually smelled, too, when he came home from work. I liked it in the store, but somehow it was different on Poppy.

Mama and Moshe walked up and down the aisles, where the canned goods and boxes were stacked on shelves like great walls. I thought the appetizing counter was much more interesting, because I could see real foods and not just pictures, and I could smell the wonderful salt herring and the lox on one end and the chocolate-covered candies on the other. When "the Partner" was behind the counter and not at the register, where he usually was, he would step around the side with his hands behind his back and smile so I could see all the black holes where his teeth belonged. Then he would say, "I know what you like, don't I?" And his voice trailed up and down as if he was singing. And then he would hold out his hands filled with chocolate-covered orange peels, and I would grab them. Mama never liked it when I took from him, so I had to do it fast.

The Partner continued in his funny singing way: "Do you know how I know what you like?" But he never waited for me to reply. "Because your poppy takes home so much of it, I know someone must like it! Every night, when he goes home, either the candies or the cookies or a herring goes home with him. Are you the lucky little girl who gets to eat it all?" I always felt uncomfortable when the Partner told me things, and I never knew how to respond, except by pretending I had to find something on the shelves and running off to the safety of the boxes and cans to eat my goodies.

One time, Mama heard our one-way conversation, and she got very angry. She took me by the wrist and pulled me out of the store. "I don't want you talking to that man," she said.

"I wasn't," I insisted.

"Or taking anything from him, either."

She pressed her lips together and said nothing more.

I couldn't imagine why she was so upset.

That night, I was dreaming that Mama was scolding me for taking a pickle in the store. She was saying, "Everything disappears. The cookies, the candy, and now the pickles." Then I realized I wasn't sleeping but that the voices I heard from the kitchen were real.

"It's not a good line of work for you. It's undignified!" Mama said.

"What's so undignified about appetizing?" Papa said. "I grant, it's not as dignified as dealing in diamonds— but we can't all be like your brother-in-law."

"Leave him out of this!" Mama raised her voice, which she hardly ever did. "He has nothing to do with this. Don't bring him into everything."

"I'm not the one bringing him in. You're the one always making comparisons. What's the matter, I don't support you in style? Would you rather, maybe, I bought you a television like your sister and then 'took off' for days on end? Hah?"

Then Mama's voice became soft, so I couldn't hear what she said, and Papa said, "The trouble is, you picked the wrong one. You had your choice, he wanted you. You should have married him if you wanted a diamond dealer. But you chose an appetizing man, so that's what you're stuck with!"

I never got scared when either of them was angry at me, because I always knew I must have done something wrong and that they were only angry for "my sake," to teach me something. But when they were angry at each other I used to picture the earth opening

27

and swallowing people up, the way the rabbi said God sometimes made it do. I worried if I was wrong to take the candy from the Partner. I didn't steal it, he gave it to me. But what did he mean by "Every day something goes home . . . the cookies, the candy, a herring"? Why was he telling that to me? Grown-ups had such strange ways of saying things. I thought about that a lot, but I still couldn't understand. For the first time, I began sensing that everyone didn't love Mama and Poppy the way I did.

After my conversation with the Partner that day, whenever we went to the store, Mama never left me by the appetizing counter except if I was talking to Poppy. She insisted I accompany her and Moshe up and down the aisles.

"I want the Partner to see that we do make purchases," she would say to us. Her voice was sharp like knives and forks clanging together. I wondered why it was so important that we show the Partner anything, since the store was half Poppy's, so we could take whatever we wanted from his share.

By the time I was in fourth grade, Mama let me go by myself to the store. She would make out a short list and send me off with two dollar bills clutched in my fist and instructions to "be sure you put the money right into Mr. Samuel's hands." I'd be half out the door when she'd call after me, "And don't take anything from him. Tell him, 'No, thank you,' if he offers." But he stopped offering. I guess he figured that, now that I was nine years old, I was a big girl and could buy my own candy.

Or maybe he thought, like Papa, that I was developing a fat tuchis from eating too much. But I loved to eat. It made me feel good, especially when I was lonely. As long as I could eat a piece of chocolate, or as long as I knew I had some cookies stashed in my pocket or hidden in a drawer waiting for me, I could get through anything. Moshe loved chocolate too. Sometimes I shared mine with him, because I felt sorry that he was stuck in the house so much because of his "delicate constitution." He was nearly six, but he still didn't go to school. A yeshiva boy came over every afternoon to teach him Hebrew, but he wasn't allowed to play in the street as I did. So I shared my cookies and my chocolate with him, and we kept it a secret, because he wasn't supposed to eat these things. Mama said they caused "inflammation of the bronchial passage."

One day, when I was in the store looking for vanilla, I noticed four cellophane-wrapped caramels on the floor. As I bent down for them, my eye fell on a one-pound bag that had been ripped open and wedged between two bags of flour in the baking-goods section. I loved caramels, with their maple flavor and intense, choking sweetness. My heart began to pound before I was even aware of what I was thinking. The bag was open anyway, so why not take a few more? But that would be stealing! No, it wouldn't! What about the candies on the floor—that wasn't stealing. But the rest of them aren't on the floor, they're in the bag. So what! If the bag should accidentally fall and the caramels spill out, they'd be on the floor, right?

No one was around. I listened for a moment. Mr. Samuel was at the register, and I knew Papa was with the cheeses. My hand reached almost by itself, and the bag slipped to the floor. The clatter startled me. But no one else heard. Half a dozen caramels scattered in the aisle. I stuffed them in my pocket. My heart was pounding against my chest as I lifted the bag and squeezed it so more would drop through the hole. I stuffed them in my pocket too. Then I ran with the bag to Mr. Samuel.

"Look what I found!" I held it up for him to inspect. I hoped he wouldn't notice my trembling. "The bag is torn and they're all falling out!" I shook it, and a dozen candies poured over the counter. Mr. Samuel extended a bony hand and pulled them toward the register; he took the bag from me and turned it over and over in his hands.

"Hoodlums!" he muttered. "Damn kids start coming in here! They do that! Let them stick to their own. They come in here looking to make trouble."

He held the bag over his head and called to Poppy.

"Peretz! Nem a kook—hoodlums!"

Then he emptied the contents into the register drawer. I must have looked disappointed. He held one out for me. "Here—take."

I grabbed it from him before he changed his mind. I was angry. I had expected he would say, "Here, take the whole bag. It's ruined anyway."

At dinner, Poppy said, "Did Miriam tell you what she discovered in the store today?"

Mama and Moshe looked at me expectantly. I grew warm all over.

"Go on, tell them, mommele." Papa smiled the way he did whenever he was about to prove a point.

"Nothing. Just an open bag of candy," I stammered.

"Hoodlums!" he exclaimed. "That's what happens once they come into a neighborhood. Vandalism—theft! Soon we'll all have to leave. Mark my words—in five years, this whole neighborhood will be shot!" I was relieved that he was so angry at the hoodlums. I was safe. But I felt guilty for keeping silent and letting him blame innocent people. I peeked at Moshe across the table, his pointy little ears taking it all in, his eyes darting from Poppy to Mama to me and back to Poppy.

Papa didn't mention the Caramel Incident again, but I kept thinking about it. I wanted more candy. I needed a scheme. I wasn't allowed to use my allowance for candy, because the school nurse wrote home that I was overweight. "Besides," Mama said, "your allowance should go for more important things." So I had to sneak the candy I bought. It made me angry that she didn't let me spend my allowance the way I wanted. The other kids bought all they wanted. They always seemed to be having such a good time. I felt that if only I could buy what they were buying, then I would be and feel just like everyone else.

The happiest hours in the day were after school, when Moshe and I ate cookies and candy and playacted the stories in the library books. Then the rest of the world disappeared; Mama used to like when we played together, because, she told us, "brothers and sisters and mamas and papas should be best friends. You can always trust your family." She taught us a little jingle:

> *Love your friends and love them well,*
> *But to your friends no secrets tell.*
> *For if your friend becomes your foe*
> *Your secrets everyone will know.*

And then she would say, "But your family you can trust, thank God. We're a very close family." I knew this was why our "family matters" were so important and so private.

I finally thought of a perfect scheme. On Wednesdays, I took Moshe to the library after school so he could listen to the Story Hour, and then we could take out as many books as our cards would allow. We always stopped on the way home to say hello to Poppy and to show him our books. I tried to sound casual as I remarked to Moshe, "I think Mama said she needed something, but I don't remember what."

Moshe looked at me kind of funny, because I never forgot these things.

"Didn't she write it down?"

"No. She was in a hurry." Then I added, "Maybe, if we walk up and down the aisles, I'll see what she wanted and remember."

"Okay." He shrugged.

I wondered if God was listening to all this, and if He would stop me at the last minute from doing what

I planned. Maybe He would strike me dead or turn me into a pillar of salt to prevent me from dragging Moshe into sin. But I tried not to think of that. Moshe always lagged behind, so I had time to reach into one of the shelves and rip a hole in a one-pound bag of M & M's.

"Do you see what I see?" I whispered to Moshe as soon as he caught up to me.

"What?" he said.

"Look—at that!" I pointed to the place where I'd put the torn bag. My hand was trembling.

Moshe walked close, squinting behind his thick horn-rimmed glasses.

"What are you talking about?" he asked.

"That bag is open!" I couldn't understand why he didn't get excited.

"So what?"

"So—nothing. It's open, that's all. It's damaged. They won't be able to sell it." I was waiting for Moshe to pick up his cue, but he lost interest and began wandering down the aisle. I reached into the shelf and pulled the bag while his back was turned. The candies scattered in the aisle. Moshe turned around. Suddenly the whole scheme seemed so obvious. What if he should realize what I'd done?

"They spilled," I said weakly.

We squatted on the floor to pick them up. Moshe started stuffing them back into the bag.

"No sense putting them back," I said. "They can't sell an open bag."

"So what should we do? It's not nice to leave a mess like this."

"We can't do that," I agreed. "Mr. Samuel might think we tore the bag."

"It's hoodlums," Moshe said. "They know it's hoodlums. They ought to call the police. Let's tell Poppy."

"No!" I said. "He'll only worry."

"So maybe we should just put it all back on the shelf and forget about it."

I was becoming exasperated with Moshe's slowness. I was afraid Mr. Samuel might have noticed us and might come looking to see what was taking us so long. My heart was pounding so hard I couldn't believe Moshe didn't hear it. Did he suspect where I was leading him?

He looked me full in the face. "What do you want to do?"

I returned his gaze but said nothing. It felt as if we had been squatting there for hours. My knees ached. If I concentrated on the ache, I wouldn't have to feel what I was saying and doing.

"Maybe we should pick it all up and put it in our pockets. We can throw it away when we get outside. Then no one has to know."

Moshe kept looking at me without changing his expression. I knew he finally understood; he would not throw the candy away once we were outside. Moshe was a practical person. He quickly swept up the pieces and began cramming them into his pockets.

"Why don't you pick them up, too?" he asked.

"I can't. My pockets have holes."

If I made the hole and took the candies, then I would be stealing. But this way it was all right.

Moshe worked quickly.

Suddenly I became aware of someone standing over us. I put my hand on Moshe's wrist to stop him. He looked at me quizzically. The presence moved closer. He wore scuffed brown shoes and baggy trousers and a long white apron. Everything inside me froze. I tried to decide whether to ignore him and hope he would go away like a bad dream or whether to greet him casually and explain about the hoodlums and not wanting to leave a mess on the floor.

Then he spoke. "What do you two think you're doing?" Mr. Samuel's European accent seemed exaggerated and sinister.

Moshe gazed at him with a sweet smile but said nothing. It was up to me to do the lying. Hot tears welled up in my eyes. I prayed they wouldn't roll down my cheeks and give me away. I had a sudden impulse to hurl myself against Mr. Samuel's legs and, weeping openly, confess my wrongdoing. I imagined him placing his large, bony hands on my head to comfort me. He would raise me up and say, "It's all right, Miriam. It's already forgiven. Don't worry. You can keep the candy, you and your brother."

But then I thought of his calling out to Papa across the store, "Peretz, nem a kook! Mach shnell! Hurry! See what angels your children are!" And Papa would put down his cheeses and come running in, and so would the customers in the store. They would all see how I had taught my brother to steal. So I decided to stick to the story about the hoodlums. But Mr. Samuel didn't care about stories.

"Empty your pockets!" he commanded.

Moshe, his smile still pasted on his lips, though his eyes were flickering with fear, dug into his jacket pockets and removed two fists full of M & M's. He deposited them, like tiny colored jewels, into Mr. Samuel's outstretched hands. As he handed them over, he looked calmly into Mr. Samuel's face and shrugged, as though to say, "There are no more. You see, I'm clean!" But he never reached into his deep trouser pockets, which were well concealed by the jacket. Mr. Samuel's gaze shifted to me.

"Where's the rest?"

I pointed to the floor where a few were left.

"What did you do—eat them all?" His eyes were riveted on my midsection, and I thought I detected a sneer. I prayed that God in His mercy would part the floorboards and swallow me up. After what seemed like a month or a year, Mr. Samuel, breathing heavily with indignation and rage, threw back his shoulders and turned from us.

"You're lucky I don't report you!' he hissed. "Get out of here—shoo! Get out!"

I grabbed Moshe by the wrist, but he jerked away from me to retrieve the candies still in the aisle. When we finally marched past the register to leave, I tried to act as though nothing had happened, but I was shaking inside. For a few minutes, my mind was a total blank as we walked, very quickly, homeward.

When we got upstairs, I went right to my room. Moshe didn't follow me to divide the candy. I didn't care. I didn't want it anyway. The less I had to do with it, the better. I just wanted to be left alone—but not to think. To sleep, to erase everything from my mind. Maybe then, when I'd wake up, I'd be a different person—a pretty me in a nice slim body with lots of friends—and different parents and no brother. *No*—how could I think such a thing? I stopped myself. I decided to take a hot bath right in the middle of the afternoon. I wanted to make myself clean inside and out, and to stop all my bad thoughts.

Moshe and I didn't play together all week. He kept himself occupied with other things when I came home from school. I missed him. I felt cut off. I read my storybooks alone, but I couldn't enjoy them. So I did my homework and went to bed early every night, which kept Mama asking, "Is everything all right? Aren't you feeling well? Do you have a fever?" I felt so cut off and alone that I couldn't even keep awake for Uncle Yitzrok's visits. I couldn't bear to face him. He would take one look at me and know what I had done. I wondered how he would respond. Somehow I felt that nothing would shock him, that Uncle Yitzrok had within himself an understanding of all deeds that man could dream of doing, the good and the evil. I almost longed for him to penetrate my secret so I wouldn't feel so alone. I hoped Moshe wouldn't tell him, for then our secret would become my shame. As long as I was the one who confessed, I could be absolved. Yet I knew I never would be.

Sunday morning, I waited nervously for Moshe's learning session with Uncle to be finished. I stood outside the door and listened as they sang together in Hebrew and Uncle related stories from the Bible more wonderful than the ones in the library books. Sometimes Uncle Yitzrok would drop his voice, and I'd hear Moshele's thin piping tones, and I knew they were confiding private things. Moshe and Uncle had a special tie, because Moshe was a boy and therefore he could be taught certain things and be expected to understand despite his being only six. There were things—about God and the nature of the universe—which would never be revealed to me. "Those things a girl doesn't need to know," Papa would say. It had been decided ever since Moshe was a baby that, as soon as he was strong enough, he would study in yeshiva. But I was sent to ordinary public school. It made me angry that no one even tried to find out if I could understand the "inner meanings," too.

After Uncle left, I approached my brother for the first time since the M & M Incident.

"Did you tell Uncle Yitzrok?" I asked.

Moshe gazed at me blankly. "Tell him what?"

"You know."

"What?"

"About last Wednesday."

"What about last Wednesday?"

I didn't understand how Moshe could have forgotten

so quickly. Perhaps he was just pretending. He did that sometimes with a straight face, so that no one could tell he was fooling around until he would suddenly erupt into peals of laughter.

I looked him in the eye.

"Did you tell him about the M & M's—you know—in Poppy's store—all over the floor?"

Moshe looked at me as though I were crazy. "What's there to tell? Some candy fell down and I picked it up. That's all."

Could it be that Moshe had not understood that he was part of my scheme? I felt relieved but also very angry. If he didn't understand, then he didn't really share the blame. It was all mine. But that wasn't fair. We both did it, and he got all the rewards. But then, why had he not spoken to me all week? It was too much to figure out.

# CHAPTER
# 6

One week later, Mama announced at dinner, "Papa and I decided it's time Moshele started yeshiva. The doctor says he's strong enough—and it's past time he started his Torah study." Moshe grinned. I glanced from Mama to Poppy. Did they think I was a bad influence on my brother? Had the Partner told Poppy, and Poppy told Mama, and that was why they decided to separate us?

Moshe slipped from his chair to hug Mama. She laughed and her face grew round and rosy. Papa smiled. Little wrinkles formed at the corners of his eyes.

"Aha!" he said. "We've got a regular Talmud chochem! Look how happy he is!"

And Mama said, "We can register him tomorrow. Then we'll buy a new suit and trousers for our little yeshiva bokher."

They were making such a fuss over Moshe, I thought of telling them about the candy incident and how Moshe was caught with his pockets full. I suspected he still had most of the M&M's hidden away somewhere, because he liked to make things last. But then I thought that either they wouldn't believe me or, more likely, they already knew and this was their way of protecting Moshele from me. I wanted to cry, "Am I such a monster that you have to separate us?" Instead, I kicked the table leg, pretending it was Moshe. I kicked it so hard that everyone's soup spilled. Papa reached over and grabbed my wrist.

"Why did you do that?" he demanded.

"It was an accident," I mumbled. He stared at me, and I knew he didn't believe me. I wanted to run to my room and slam the door and throw myself on my bed, but Papa was gripping my wrist.

"Clean up that mess." He spoke softly, but it sounded angry. It sounded as though he were accusing me of every crime in the world. He let go of my wrist, and I went to the sink and tore off some paper towels and got the sponge and sopped up the mess, and then Mama ladled more soup into everyone's bowl.

All through dinner, the conversation revolved around Moshele's entrance into yeshiva. I wanted to say or do something to let them know I still existed, but I couldn't think of anything, so I settled for taking seconds and then thirds of the cheesecake Poppy had brought home from the store.

The next afternoon, Mama was beaming when I came home from school.

"They sent him right into a class," she said proudly. "As soon as he was registered, they called a monitor to take him to Bible Study. I have to pick him up at four."

I had hoped he'd be home earlier and we could play

together. The house seemed empty and quiet. I went to my room and spread my books on my desk, but I couldn't concentrate. I kept trying to imagine what Moshe was doing. I lay on my bed, and the next thing I heard was light rapping on the door and Moshe calling, "Sissa— Sissa! I'm home! Come look at all my books!"

They were piled high on his table in the alcove. A blue pencil case with a Mogen David lay on his bed beside the table. The books were old, shabby, well worn, and well used by generations of little Torah scholars. No pictures to whet the imagination. Only endless close-knit lines of ancient Hebrew lettering. I could read some Hebrew from Sunday school. I'd learned to make the appropriate sound to correspond with the mysterious little slashes and dots and curlicues that appeared on the pages but had never learned what anything meant. I was taught that Hebrew was God's language, and I wondered if that was why it was impossible to understand. I knew Uncle Yitzrok derived hidden meanings from the strange markings and that he was teaching these meanings to Moshe. I knew that when Moshe read the Hebrew, he would understand the mysteries that were locked to me.

When I used to ask Papa about sending me to yeshiva so I, too, could understand, he'd say, "What they teach you in public school is enough. A girl doesn't need to know more, she doesn't need yeshiva. You'll get married, your husband will learn. It's enough." And Mama would say, "You should only live and be well and graduate high school and find a good husband, an observant man, please God. That's all we ask. We'll be proud of you."

But I wanted them to ask more; I wanted them to expect as much from me as from Moshe.

I thumbed through some of the books, feigning interest. I was surprised and delighted when he turned to me suddenly and whispered, "Let's go in your room and read the library books." So we sat down on my bed and closed the door and opened a book between us, but as soon as we came to those magical words, my favorite words in the whole language, "Once upon a time . . ." two tears fell on the page. I looked at Moshe, and he flung his arms around my neck. I held him close. and we rocked back and forth as Mama used to do with me. I wanted to hold him that way forever, to feel his chest against mine and his breath on my neck. But after a while I felt his muscles tense, and he pulled back from me. He stared down at the floor as he spoke.

"I don't want to go to yeshiva! They're all bigger than me and they talk fast, and I don't understand! Please, Sissa, can't I come home and play with you? I like the library books better!"

I couldn't understand why he was asking my permission. Didn't he know it wasn't up to me—that I also wanted him home? It was Mama and Papa who were separating us. Mama, Papa, and Torah.

There was a light *rat-tat-tat* on the door, and Mama called, "Moshele! Come have something to eat and do your homework!" Her voice was filled with smiles and pride. Moshe sighed and slid off the bed and walked to the door without looking back.

That night, as I lay in bed, I heard his sobbing in the other room.

After that, when he came home from school, he went straight to his study table and opened his books without a word. When I passed through the living room, I saw him poring over volumes that seemed bigger than he was. He hunched his shoulders over the page, gently rocking back and forth as he chanted his lessons in an undertone. Sometimes he paused and straightened up, removed his glasses, and rubbed his eyes with his fists.

I had strict orders not to disturb my brother when he was working, which seemed to be all the time. Sometimes an older student came home with him, and they sat at the table and learned together. If I had to pass by, I'd walk on tippy-toes and pretend not to notice them. I felt that Moshe was hardly my brother anymore. He'd been taken away from me.

As winter slipped into early spring and, outside, the ice and snow were melting, and everything smelled fresh and alive, inside, Moshe seemed to be slipping farther from me. He hardly spoke at the dinner table except to recite his lessons to Mama and Poppy. He had two tiny worry lines between his brows like an old man, but nobody seemed to notice. One time, when I passed him on the way to the bathroom, I asked, "Do you want to come look at the library book with me?"

"No time—I'm too busy," he mumbled without looking up.

I thought there was anger in his voice. When I had passed, he called after me, "Sissa!"

I turned.

He shrugged. "Never mind. There's no time." And I saw that the anger was mingled with a great sadness. It seemed too much for such a little boy. I wanted to hold him, but he had already returned to his desk.

# CHAPTER
## 7

We had one last big snowfall even though it was nearly spring. Then it turned freezing cold again.

"You want to go ice-skating tomorrow in Prospect Park?" Rosie asked.

I'd never been ice-skating, but it sounded exciting.

"If Mama will let me."

"Why shouldn't she let you?"

"I don't know." I was never quite sure of Mama's reasons for things. So I was pleasantly surprised when all she said was, "Be very careful you don't fall down. And dress warm. Here, I'll give you some money; how much is it?"

"I don't know."

"Ask Rosie."

"Okay."

"And I'll give you a thermos of something hot, you shouldn't catch cold."

"Okay."

I could hardly sleep that night, thinking about how it would be skating on ice with Rosie. Then I thought that Mama was probably glad to have me out of the house on Sunday so Moshe could concentrate better.

Since Moshe's entrance into yeshiva, I was spending more time than ever with Rosie. I missed Moshele terribly, but when I was with Rosie it wasn't so bad.

When we got to the rink, it was already packed. I recognized a lot of kids from school right away. Blue jackets, red scarves, brightly colored woolen hats whizzed by me as I peered across the railing. It looked so easy. Even little children darted in and out between the other skaters. Light dustings of snow formed soft ridges here and there, especially around the railing. The wind stung my cheeks. I was anxious to put on skates and enter the fun.

We pushed our way into the skate house and over to the counter to make our rentals. There was a small space on the bench, and Rosie and I wedged ourselves into it. Someone gave me a dirty look. Rosie stood up— she looked so slim and elegant on the skates. I half expected her to do a pirouette right there in the skate house. I stood, too. A sharp pain shot though my ankles, as I teetered, nearly losing my balance. The boots felt too tight. My legs ached. And when I started to follow Rosie out to the rink, I wobbled and bumped into people.

Rosie presented her ticket and set foot on the ice immediately.

I hesitated.

"Come on, don't be afraid!" she called to me as she skated away.

I clutched the side railing, my legs starting to slip uncontrollably as soon as my blades touched the ice.

"Hey—look who's trying to skate!" I recognized the voice from school. "Come on, Blubber, let's see what you can do!" Then a bunch of higher-pitched giggles from the girls in back of Harry. I knew them all from my classes or from the schoolyard. I was sorry I had come with Rosie. Ice-skating wasn't for me; I was too fat. Besides, I wasn't with Rosie, after all. I'd thought we'd be holding hands, skating together, but she was on the opposite side of the rink talking to two of her other friends. I felt abandoned. I had to struggle to hold back my tears.

"Yoo-hoo! Blubber-puss!" My schoolmates had circled the rink and returned. "Give it a try—what are you afraid of?"

I clutched the railing tighter. My legs began slipping out again. No, please, God, don't let me fall—not now! Please! The next moment, I was sitting on the ice. The impact was stunning—in my pain I almost forgot my schoolmates standing over me, jeering. I tried to get up, but kept flopping back onto the ice. Finally, an instructor came and pulled me up.

"Boy, he must be strong to pull that thing off the ice!" I heard Harry laugh as the whole bunch of them skated off.

"I'm never going skating again," I promised myself. Just then Rosie came over to me. Her two friends glided up behind her.

"Miriam, we decided to go for pizza. You want to come?"

Rosie knew pizza wasn't kosher.

"No, thanks," I said.

"Okay. We're gonna go now. Enjoy your skating!"
She turned and called back, "Maybe I'll come over
later, after supper!"

Then she was gone. I felt ashamed to let them see
me leaving the ice right after they did, so I continued
clutching the rail till after they left the skate house.
Then I hobbled off the ice, returned my skates, and left
too.

Oh, why couldn't I be with Moshele now? Why
couldn't we do everything together? He never hurt me.

# CHAPTER
# 8

Whenever Uncle Yitzrok came over, Papa brought out the schnapps. Mama looked at Uncle sharply.

"Yitzrok, you shouldn't be drinking like that!" She sounded as though she were scolding both Uncle and Papa. Uncle laughed.

"Why not? You don't see me drunk, do you? A man works hard, he gets no other satisfactions. He needs a little schnapps in his system. Zeher gut!" Then he looked at Mama as though he was telling her something that only she could understand. She turned away from him. He held his schnapps toward the light and watched the colors dancing in the glass. He was quiet a long time, and I thought he must have forgotten about Mama and their conversation. But then he sighed deeply and leaned back in his chair.

"Schnapps!" he said. And he began to laugh, though I couldn't understand what was funny. "It's a mystical experience! It's the only way some people get to see God."

I wondered what that meant. What did God have to do with it? Did he actually see the Face of God, which was forbidden for man to look upon? Was the Face in the shimmering golden pink of the schnapps?

Mama said, "And do you see God, Yitzrok?"

Uncle thought a minute and then said, "Sometimes. Sometimes I do."

"I don't think you do," Mama said. "I think you're deceiving yourself, Yitzrok. I think you're seeking in the wrong places."

Then no one spoke for a long while. I wanted a cookie, but I was afraid they would notice me and send me away if I reached for one, so I kept still.

When Uncle continued, he was no longer laughing and smiling. "Oh? And where should I look? I come here to drink schnapps. Here, in your house, because it's a nice religious home, a kosher home. I can feel the keddushah, the holiness here. So maybe it's both, the schnapps and being here. Maybe this is where I look for God."

I wondered what he would think if he knew what I had done, of the sin I had brought upon the family. How could he find God in such a home? Would he stop coming to visit?

Mama said, "You're drunk. Go home."

"I'm not drunk. But I'll leave if you want me to." He sat perfectly still and looked Mama in the eye. Mama avoided his stare. She remained silent a long while before she said, "It's all right, you can stay."

Then he said, "My wife tells you I go off drinking for days at a time?"

"She doesn't tell me anything."

"Because it's not true. Here is the only place I drink. Here—and for holy purposes. There's nothing for me

51

in a bar—with goyim. But I'll tell you—I do go off to search for God."

"I don't understand you, Yitzrok. You frighten me. You never used to talk like this."

"I don't expect you to understand." He poured himself another drink. Papa got up and put the bottle back in the pantry. Uncle Yitzrok leaned his elbows on the table and rested his forehead in his palms. He closed his eyes and clutched his hair, squeezing it with his long fingers as though trying to extract the words he needed.

"Some people find God in family life. The family— that's keddushah! Or they make Shabbos, and they find Him there. But some people don't. They can't. So they have to look elsewhere."

The intensity in Uncle Yitzrok's voice and the sadness in his eyes drew me to him. I didn't understand what he was saying, but I felt he was hurting, and I wanted to go to him and put my arms around his neck and tell him I felt his sadness and that I understood, but I did not know what it was I understood.

Uncle's visits were the highlight of the day. Mama usually let me stay in the kitchen and listen to their talk, as long as Uncle Yitzrok didn't start "drinking too much," and as long as I'd finished my homework. Uncle was fond of telling parables and tales, of which he had an endless store. He would stretch his legs forward and tilt so far back in his chair that Mama occasionally started as though to catch him. He would fold his arms behind his head, his eyelids gently closed, and remain silent an instant, as though he were receiving divine inspiration.

Then a smile would brighten his face. He would sigh or, occasionally, chuckle and begin.

"There was once a very poor peasant . . ." or "In the magnificent court of the Rebbe of . . ." or "In the days of the Czar, they should never come again, lived two ancient Jews. . . ."

His favorite parables were about Shabbos. He liked the ones that compared the wise servant who made ample preparations when advised that the Queen would visit and so won her favor with the foolish servant who did very little. Then, depending on whether he'd already had two or three drinks of schnapps, he would remain silent at the end and allow us to draw our own inferences, or else he would laugh or groan, I couldn't tell which, with a single, sharp "Aha!" and, turning to me, add, "So you see how it is, mommele." Or not turn to me at all but address himself to the room at large or to some invisible spirit with whom he seemed to be communing. "How can one receive the Queen properly when one's wife refuses to dust or to set out a tablecloth, or she leaves pencils and money lying around?" If he carried on longer than this about Tante Sophie, Mama would send me from the room.

One evening, he came when Papa had to stay late at the store. Mama poured him a cup of tea and brought out the cookies. He stirred and stirred the tea, till I thought he was composing a melody of tinkles, perhaps something we could sing on Shabbos. I pulled my chair up close, since there were only three of us and I didn't feel I had to take "my place" as a child in a room of grown-ups. When he stopped stirring, everything suddenly became silent. He lifted his head to speak, and I knew he was about to tell me something wonderful.

"Shabbos—" he said. I waited for more, but he withdrew into himself until I began to doubt that he had said anything at all. But then he repeated, "Shabbos—" and he gestured toward the ceiling as though the day were hovering over our heads. He sighed and continued.

"I remember Shabbosim, Friday nights, at your mama's house. Remember, Sarah?"

Mama got a funny look on her face, as though responding to a quick stab of pain.

"Please, Yitzrok. Don't," she said. But he didn't hear her.

"I remember watching you light the candles. Your face—your whole body, your shoulders—were infused with—holiness, with light. You were the most beautiful—"

"Please, Yitzrok. Miriam—"

"I'm just talking about Shabbos, Sarah. There's nothing she can't hear. To me—you were the incarnation of Shabbos, the Queen, the Bride. I looked forward to a lifetime of Shabbats—until the gallant Prince Peretz came along and swept you away."

Mama had turned away from us both.

Uncle Yitzrok made one of his loud "Ahas!" and then added, "You see, mommele, I talk wilder, I talk stranger things when I drink tea than when I drink

54

schnapps. So you mustn't pay attention. I'm drunk on words. It doesn't mean anything."

He lowered his gaze and stared into his lap. When it began to seem he might sit there like stone all night, Mama got up from the table and went to the stove for the kettle. She poured him another cup of tea. He looked up at her like a helpless puppy. He rested his hand on hers to stop her from pouring.

"Not this," he whispered. "Not tea. You know what I need."

For an instant, Mama looked as though she might drop the kettle, but then she turned toward the stove to put it back. Only he held on to her arm so she couldn't go.

"Please—Sarah!"

I became frightened. I'd never heard such urgency in anyone's voice.

Mama pulled her arm from him with a sharp movement, so that some of the tea spurted out of the spout and scalded her.

"Go home, Yitzrok." Her voice was soft and unnaturally controlled. "Go home."

Uncle remained as he was, uncomprehending or deaf. Then he burst into his "Aha!" and a long, forced laugh. Mama didn't seem amused. I wanted to run from the room. I felt there was something terrible going on that I could not understand and did not want to. I wanted to run to Moshe and wake him, to hold him in my arms and pretend there were just the two of us. But I didn't want to leave Mama.

"Some schnapps, please! You know what I need, Sarah. Please—some schnapps!" Mama didn't budge. He made his sound again, but this time his "Aha!" sounded more like a cry than a laugh. A cry from the bowels of the earth.

"A little schnapps!" he repeated. "What did you think I meant?" But Mama still didn't budge or acknowledge that she'd heard him. He withdrew then into silence—and after a few moments, he arose abruptly and walked to the door.

"I better go now," he said, as though the idea had just occurred to him. He closed the door quietly behind him.

Mama remained frozen, staring after the figure at the door long after he had gone. I thought of going to her, but she seemed so remote—not like Mama at all. It was as if I had suddenly glimpsed something in her that changed everything—but I didn't know what it was or what was the meaning of the change.

After what seemed like an eternity, she noticed me. "Go to bed, Miriam." Her voice was hollow and hoarse. She didn't call me "mommele" but "Miriam"—as though I were a stranger to her. I turned and went to my room, not daring to even breathe "Good night" to her.

Alone, I undressed in the dark. I didn't want to expose my thoughts or my tangled feelings. I didn't want to have to look at them. I crawled into bed without washing, without saying my prayers or even remembering to bless God. I was grateful for the comforting weight of the covers as they settled over me. I remembered Uncle saying that, when he disappeared, he was going in search of God. I tried to imagine how he did this—how I would do such a thing—but I could not. I was confused. I was taught that God is everywhere, in all things. So why did Uncle have to go somewhere else in order to look for him? I felt as if I were sinking into the earth. I was grateful for no more thoughts or feelings.

# CHAPTER
## 9

After that night, we didn't see Uncle Yitzrok for a whole month. When Papa said, "It looks like your brother-in-law took off again!" Mama remained silent. I felt sorry for Moshe when Uncle didn't come around. Sunday mornings, when they sang and learned together, were the only times Moshe smiled. It was during that month that Moshe confided in me that Uncle had been teaching him the hidden meanings.

"Everything has meaning that we don't know about," he said. "Torah especially. You can't just study what's there. You have to go deeper. That's where Uncle goes when he takes off. To seek out the mysteries."

"But where does he go?" I asked.

Moshe shrugged. "I don't know. But he promised that someday, when I know enough Torah and I'm old enough to understand, he'll take me with him."

"Is that where he is now?"

"Of course it is. Only I wish he'd come back."

Moshe seemed so certain of himself, I was tempted to believe him. Only I couldn't help feeling that, this time, Uncle's disappearance had something to do with Mama.

I was sensing that both Mama and Moshe were connected to Uncle Yitzrok in ways that had "deeper meanings" and in which I was not included. The stories he told at the kitchen table were no longer enough for me. I wanted to be taken into his mysteries. I thought about Uncle Yitzrok a lot. I wondered if Rosie knew his secret.

One afternoon, when we were in her room, I asked her.

She shrugged. "I don't know. He doesn't say."

"Don't you miss him when he takes off?"

She shrugged again. I thought she seemed bored with the conversation.

"When he's home, they only argue, anyway."

"But don't you miss him?" I persisted. "If my papa disappeared—"

Rosie turned away. She started fixing her hair. I was afraid I had made her feel bad, so I kept still. After a while, she whispered, "Sometimes I think about him. On Shabbos . . ." But then she continued fixing her hair, and she didn't speak again. So I just sat on her bed and watched her until it began getting dark. Then I hugged her to say good night, and she began to cry. We both cried and held each other for a long time.

A few nights later, I was awakened by the sound of arguing in the kitchen. As soon as I recognized Uncle Yitzrok's voice, I got excited. He had come back. Now he was in our apartment. I tried to make out what they were saying.

"It would be only for a few days, Sarah. Just so he

can see what it's like being with people who spend an hour a day talking to God—actually talking to Him—out loud. Without shame or embarrassment."

Then Mama said, "He's serious enough."

And Papa said, "He's too serious. He does his davening. That's his talking to God. It's enough."

And Uncle said, "It's not enough. What they teach in traditional yeshivas, it's not enough. They don't penetrate—they don't go deep—"

"It's enough, it's enough," Papa said.

Uncle was nearly shouting. "The psalmist says, 'I cried unto the Lord and He healed me!' That's what these people do—they pour out their hearts to God. He heals them. Moshe can be healed, too. Crying to God—it strengthens, it heals!"

Then Mama said something about being "off the deep end," and Papa said something about schnapps. And Mama said, "Leave the schnapps alone."

I wondered if Moshe was also awake and listening. He might be frightened by hearing Uncle shout and by hearing them talk about him. I waited until their voices were raised again, and then I tiptoed into the living room, where Moshe slept. He was sitting up in bed. I sat down beside him and put my arm around him, and we listened together.

"You see only the outside shell of things," Uncle was saying. "You miss the inner sparks."

"He can learn about the sparks when he's older," Papa said. "The sparks can wait."

"They can't wait!"

Then Mama said, "Yitzrok, the matter is closed."

And Papa said, "Wait till he's bar mitzvah. Then you can teach him these things."

Moshe's eyes grew wide.

Mama said, "Peretz!" She sounded angry.

Papa said, "You can ask again then. Maybe we'll let him go—maybe. But not before!"

Uncle said, "It can't wait six years!" And Mama said, "It will have to—if we let him go at all. If! We're not promising anything."

And Uncle said, "I'm disappointed. I thought you would understand." Then they lowered their voices, and we couldn't make out what they were saying.

"Where does he want to take you?" I whispered.

"I don't know. I think it's somewhere in Brooklyn. Williamsburg, maybe. Or else it's Eretz Yisroel."

"Eretz Yisroel! You think so?"

How wonderful for my brother to be going to the Holy Land! I wished I could go with him.

After a while, we heard the dishes clinking, and we knew Mama was clearing the table. We heard Papa's voice and Mama's but not Uncle Yitzrok's. He must have gone home. I hadn't heard the door close, but it wouldn't have surprised me if Uncle was able to slip into and out of places by penetrating them with his presence—like the angels, who had no need of doors. I left Moshe, to return to my own room before I was discovered.

# CHAPTER
# 10

Two nights later, there was a wild pounding on the door. I sat up in bed, my heart racing. I thought I was having a nightmare. We had been reading about the Holocaust in history; perhaps this was more of it—shrill voices, incoherent crying, shuffling of feet in the kitchen.

By this time, I was out of bed. I met Moshe, blind without his glasses, outside my room. He threw his arms around me and buried his head in my stomach. I comforted him with, "Shhh . . . shhh . . . na-na . . . tsk-tsk-tsk, it's all right," just as Mama used to do for me.

Tante Sophie was pacing back and forth between the couch and the dining table. Cousin Rosie followed, tugging at her sleeves. Their faces were streaked with tears, their hair wild, and their nightgowns hung out beneath their coats. Everyone was screaming at once. Tante Sophie fell into Mama's arms. Rosie was crying, "Please! Mama, please! Stop it!" Papa was shouting, "What's the matter, Sophie? Tell us—what's the matter?" Only Mama spoke softly: "Let her sit down, Peretz. Let her catch her breath." Tante let Mama push her into a chair, but she was still hysterical. And Rosie kept repeating,

"Mama, please!" She seemed not to see me or Moshe or any of us, only her mama. Papa grew impatient. "Will you kindly tell us what's wrong!" He placed himself squarely in front of her. But Mama pushed him gently out of the way as she approached her sister and drew her close. She held Tante's head against her, stroking her hair until Tante's breath came easily enough to make her words comprehensible.

"Tell me—please! I beg you! Where is he? Please—"

"What are you talking about?" Mama asked.

"So! He's taken off again, eh? So what else is new?" Papa said.

"Peretz!" Mama looked at him warningly.

"Not 'again'!" Tante cried. "For good! Fartik! Kaput!" And she thrust a wrinkled piece of paper into Mama's hand.

Rosie murmured, "Oh, Mama, Mama! He'll come back!" But her eyes begged my mama for a response, as though Mama could bring relief.

I wanted to run to Rosie, but I felt I mustn't leave Moshe. I sensed he was looking to me for protection and strength.

Mama stared at the note. Her face was immobile. She handed the paper to Papa.

Tante looked anxiously from one to the other. "Please. Tell me where he is."

"I don't know where he is," Mama said.

Papa shoved the note back at Sophie. "How should we know where he went?" he asked. "You think he tells us these things? That's his business!"

"But he said—the note says, 'Sarah will know how to reach me.' He's never said that before."

Moshe's eyes caught mine. I could sense he was holding his breath, as though he felt his entire future was on the line.

"I don't know, I don't know," Mama repeated.

Then Papa said, "Why do you come screaming, hysterical in the middle of the night? You could have come earlier. You knew he was gone."

"It's all right, Peretz. Leave her alone."

"No! I want to know—why does she wake us up like this? He's taken off before."

"No! This is different!" And Tante began to weep again.

"It is different," Rosie whispered.

"This time I know—it's for good. He's not coming back."

"How do you know?"

"I know, I know."

"But I don't know how to reach him," Mama said. "I don't know where he is, believe me."

"Put an ad in the Public Notices section—"

"So all the neighbors will find out! It's none of their business! This is a family matter."

"So—don't put an ad in." Papa shrugged. "I'm only trying to be helpful. Don't put an ad in."

"Won't you tell me anything?" Tante pulled away from Mama. Her voice was much calmer now. They were two sisters talking together. "I'm sorry, Sarah—I'm sorry—for anything I ever said that hurt you. Forgive me. I get excited easily, you know that. I'm high-strung. But I'm sorry if I provoked—"

"You don't have to apologize, Sophie. If I had any information, I'd tell you without your apologizing. But I don't."

"Is it the things I said about Shabbos? Or religion? I didn't say them to hurt you. It's just—"

"I know you didn't. But can't you understand, I simply don't know where Yitzrok is. He doesn't tell me these things."

Tante smiled bitterly. I'd never seen such an expression on her face.

"Then what kind of things does he tell you, Sarah?"

Mama pressed her lips together and turned her face away.

"Your husband is a mystic," Papa declared. "A religious mystic. You know that. He probably went . . . searching. He'll be back. He's just—"

"Searching? Searching for what? What's there to search for?"

I recalled Uncle's words: "Some people find God in family life. The family—that's keddushah! Or they make Shabbos and they find Him there. But some people don't. They can't. So they have to look elsewhere."

Moshe began to withdraw. Singing and chanting Torah were no longer his solace. Silence was.

He sat at the dinner table and didn't say a word. He hardly touched his food. Mama would spend entire afternoons simmering and baking and steaming his favorite kugels and desserts, only to see them grow cold in front of him. Sometimes he picked at a few raisins or a noodle on his plate. As soon as Mama allowed him, he made his blessings and left the table to return to his studies. I didn't think it was possible for anyone to be thinner than Moshe, yet every day he seemed closer to transparency. And when he had one of his coughing fits, I would picture his body, flimsily constructed on a toothpick frame instead of bone, being hacked into splinters and scattered in the wind. I associated his thinness with his spirituality, as though he were preparing his body for flight to heaven. Whenever I was near him, my own body weighed heavily on me. I felt locked into my earthiness. I might serve to lift him up from my position down below, but I would never soar alongside him.

# CHAPTER
# 11

One Friday afternoon, as I was helping Mama scrape and cut carrots for our Shabbos tsimmes, she said, "You know, it's a great mitzvah for sisters and brothers to share with each other." She turned from the stove and gazed steadily at me. Usually, she talked without looking up from whatever she was doing, so I knew this conversation was special. The challahs had just come out of the oven, and their sweet, yeasty aroma filled the kitchen. Mama wiped her hands on her apron, and she walked to the table where I was sitting. She brushed back a lock of hair that had fallen over my eye. Her hand was soft and moist, just as it was when I was a little girl and she used to hold me. She hardly ever touched me anymore, I suppose because she felt I was grown up now and didn't need it.

Then she said, "Your brother is getting to be a big boy. He needs a little space for himself. Your papa and I would like for you to share your room with him. We'll put up a partition so you'll each have your privacy."

My room! It was the only thing I had that was all mine. I would be happy to share anything else with Moshe. But not my room! I felt tears spring into my eyes. I was ashamed of my selfishness and angry at Mama and Papa. They shouldn't ask me to make this sacrifice. Moshe always got everything!

Mama said, "Don't cry, mommele. I know it's a lot to ask. But you're a big girl, and we know you can make the adjustment." She gave me a quick hug and returned to the stove as though the matter was closed. Whenever they wanted me to give something up, they reminded me of what a "big girl" I was. I felt as though I was being tricked.

Mama continued: "We saw a nice plastic partition on Thirteenth Avenue. It's solid like a wall and will go all the way to the ceiling. They have one stained to look like wood. We thought that one would be very nice for your room. After Shabbos, you can come look at it. Maybe you'll see another one you like better. We'll leave it up to you."

They had it all planned. I wondered if they'd already told Moshe and if I was the last one to find out.

Mama set the pot of peas in front of me for shelling. Whenever she sensed I was about to complain, she would thrust a chore into my hands—some onions for chopping or a slab of flanken and the special basin we used for salting and soaking meat in accordance with the laws of kashrut. And I would bring the meat and the basin to the sink and take down the big red-and-yellow box of "coarse salt for koshering" from the shelf, while Mama tied the "meat apron" around my waist, giving me a quick squeeze as she did. "Ken-eine ha'ra," she would murmur. Literally, "May the evil one not . . ."

But the hug really meant, "Don't dwell on your complaints, sheine mommele. Just pick yourself up and do a mitzvah." And she would give me a gentle shove toward the sink or the table. Doing mitzvoth, fulfilling God's Commandments, was Mama's solution for everything. She was always tending to some sick neighbor or sending me on errands for them. And the entire week was laced with "mitzvoth for the Shabbos"—cleaning and polishing the candle holders, washing the lace shawl she reserved for draping over her head when she kindled and blessed the lights; or she would send me to a particular store to buy the greens or the parsnips for the soup or sesame seeds to enhance the challah. No effort was too great for Shabbos, nor any detail too small. The other six days served only as preparation for the seventh. In this way, Mama managed to turn off the problems as they arose during the week. It was only during the week right after Uncle Yitzrok disappeared that I sensed Mama's sadness despite her mitzvoth.

Sunday afternoon, we ordered the partition. When we came home from the store, Mama and Papa helped me move my things to one side of the room. Moshe was getting the windows; because of his weak eyes, he needed the better light for studying. I got the door side. We left a narrow passage for Moshe. Mama gave me some white chiffon to make a curtain for privacy.

When they started dragging Moshe's things into the room—his study table, a chair, a nightstand for his medicines and his lamp, everything but his bed—I walked into the kitchen because I was so angry I felt it coming out of me—I pictured myself erupting, as I'd seen in photographs of Mount Vesuvius. So I sat in the kitchen by myself and ate cookies till I felt better.

Monday, after supper, two men from the store came to put up the partition. Mama made Moshe wait till Tuesday before he moved in "in order to let the dust settle." There was no dust as far as I could see; she was just being extra cautious, as she always was with Moshe.

As I lay in bed that night, I felt closed in, as though I were in a closet or worse. I pictured myself in a long, narrow casket without space to stretch my arms and legs and without air. I felt my throat close up. I buried my head in the pillow so no one would hear me crying.

Moshe was very quiet. The only sound from his side was the hollow, high-pitched rattle of his breathing and the occasional creaking of his chair. I kept waiting for him to do or to say something so I could complain that he wasn't letting me sleep. I was distracted by his being so close. I wanted to talk to him, to touch him. I felt the partition was separating me from myself. I longed to connect, as though touching him would in some way assure my wholeness. But apparently Moshe didn't need the connection. He was immersed in his studies. The density of his concentration was palpable. Moshe's studies seemed to lift him out of this world. I had a sense of him rising, weightless, from his chair, floating over Brooklyn, rendezvousing in some mystical way with Uncle Yitzrok. I was sure they were communing with each other. Torah was their medium. I could feel Uncle Yitzrok's presence, though it was for Moshe and not

70

for me. They existed together in a realm that was deep and wonderful and held all the secrets of the universe. I closed my eyes as though that would bring me closer to the mystery. Moshe began chanting. I knew it was psalms, though I couldn't make out which one, because his voice was so soft. I felt myself swaying gently to his incantations, as though it were I who was praying. After a while, he finished. I heard him close his book. Then he sighed as though he were casting off the burdens of the day. His chair creaked, then scraped the floor as he stood. He was reciting the Evening Prayers: "He, being merciful, forgives iniquity and does not destroy. . . . Blessed art Thou, Lord our God, King of the Universe. . . ." I stood, too, and recited with him, so that our prayers might ascend together.

# CHAPTER
# 12

With Moshe firmly entrenched in his studies, Rosie became dearer to me than ever. I could scarcely wait for Shabbos, because we always spent the whole day together. Rosie was the most exciting person in my life. She knew all sorts of things, which I imagined she learned from hanging around with ninth graders (even though she was only in eighth grade, one year ahead of me) and from watching lots of television and movies and reading the popular magazines of which Mama and Papa disapproved. Rosie subscribed to *Seventeen*; she let me borrow her copies when she was through with them, but I had to keep them hidden in my drawer, so Mama wouldn't find them. I admired the way Rosie dressed. Tante let her wear nylon stockings and lipstick, though Mama usually frowned when she showed up in our house on Shabbos "all decked out."

Rosie and I talked about everything when we were alone together. Some of her views startled me and left me confused and churning inside for days. Like the conversation that started off being about shul but soon diverged so that I felt my whole orientation toward the world was being challenged. We were taking our Shabbos afternoon stroll when Rosie, who had seemed angry all morning, declared, "One of these days I'm going to find myself a shul where men and women are treated equally. I'm sick of sitting in the back all the time like a second-class citizen. I'd like to find a place of worship where not only men and women but Jews and Christians are treated as equals. Where Christians aren't looked down upon as goyim. Where it's okay to love and marry whom you please!"

Mama had always warned me that "marrying a goy" would be the one most unforgivable sin I could commit. That, and failing to "honor" my parents. "Besides," Mama had said, "goyim don't make good husbands. They drink too much. They don't respect their wives." Assimilation and Israel were about the only topics, aside from the store, local gossip, and our own family concerns, that I'd ever heard Mama and Papa discuss. And their views were so staunch that I couldn't imagine any decent Jew feeling otherwise. I must have seemed terribly naïve when I blurted, "But—that's assimilation!" because Rosie laughed as she replied, "So what? I think we should assimilate. What's so great about holding ourselves apart, as though we're better than everyone else?"

"Would you marry one of them?"

"Of course. That is, if I choose to marry at all—and that's a big if."

"Don't you want to?"

It had never occurred to me that a woman, especially

a Jewish woman, might not want to marry. Marriage and children were our destiny, I had thought.

"Why should I? Unless maybe he was black. In black families, the woman is in charge. And that would provide a good in for working in the Black Power movement."

I knew Rosie was involved with some high school kids in a political club, but she'd been very secretive about it. Now the pieces seemed to come together. I was both shocked and intrigued that Rosie, my own cousin, my best friend, could hold such anarchistic views. I, too, bristled under the unfairness of a system which automatically favored my brother over me simply because he was a boy. But I'd never dared question it, because I'd been taught—and I believed—that this was as God meant it to be. I admired Rosie greatly for her outspokenness. But I was still taken aback by the lengths to which she'd be willing to go.

"Would you really marry a shvartzer?"

"Don't call them that. Shvartz is derogatory."

"No, it isn't. Shvartz means black. That's what everyone calls them."

"Then call them black. Don't use Yiddish code words. You're not living in a European shtetl. You live in America—speak English!"

I felt put down and ashamed of all I clung to that was Jewish, in the old way that Rosie and the outside world looked upon as "old-fashioned" or "ghetto-type" Jews.

Rosie's anger seemed so sharp, I wondered if she

wasn't being cut by it, too.

After that, I became very quiet. She must have sensed my withdrawal, for we finished our walk in silence.

But usually Shabbos, from beginning to end, was a much more peaceful occasion.

Friday afternoons, Papa and Moshe went to shul. I liked being alone with Mama in the house, even though we were both rushing to get ready for Shabbos on time.

"Miriam—what's keeping you?"

Mama was ready to light the candles. I couldn't zip up my dress. It was always something. The Friday before, my hair was knotted, and I couldn't get the comb through it, and the week before that, I'd forgotten to polish my shoes until the last minute. Mama almost lit the candles without me. I had started dressing extra early this time, when the zipper got stuck. Papa said I was so clumsy because of my size. "If she didn't have such a gantze tuchis, maybe she'd be able to move faster!" But Mama said it was only baby fat and I'd outgrow it. I wished I were more like Moshe. No one ever had to wait for him. I supposed that was because he was so skinny he could move faster, and also because he was so smart.

I couldn't force the zipper any farther, so I arranged my hair to hide where the dress remained open. Then I joined Mama at the dining table.

Twilight filled the room, separating the Shabbos from the six working days, shielding us from the din of the outside world, drawing us together for the coming of the Shechina, God's Spirit. All my cares drained out of me. It was a warm, melting sensation, as though my very flesh were falling, falling from my bones. And when Mama kindled the lights, I felt drawn into a time that was beyond time. It was something so special that, though I shared it with Mama, I never spoke about it— I preferred to savor and preserve the moment for myself. Yet I knew that Mama understood, that she experienced it, too—and that, because of this one moment each week, she loved me in a way my brother and even Papa would never know.

Saturday morning was different from any other morning. We all dressed up to go to shul, where we met everyone we didn't get to see during the week. Rosie and I and Mama and Tante Sophie sat together in the women's section. It was the only time of the week that Mama and Tante didn't argue. After services, we would walk home, Rosie and I a block or so ahead of our parents, always under their distant supervision. "Wait for the light! Girls, watch how you cross!" or "Miriam, put your hat back on—it's still March!" Yet we were alone, and together we shared solemn secrets, we hummed and harmonized our favorite hymns, we made up games, and we wove stories using special code words so no one could penetrate our private world. We giggled and we held hands. Angels danced between us.

Shabbos lunch was the most special meal of the week. After the meal, the little green books with the Hebrew songs and blessings were distributed, and Moshe, his study partner, Yussele, Rosie, and I would vie with each other for calling out the numbers of our favorite zmirot for all to sing. Mama would bring a platter of cinnamon-and-raisin ruggelach or fudge brownies and set it down before us; the rose porcelain teapot would make its appearance on a round petaled coaster, along with the jar of honey and the plate of lemon slices. Cups and spoons tinkled their accompaniment to our voices. Then we sang the grace, and the family dispersed—my brother and Yussele to pore over the laws of Shabbos on the living-room sofa, Mama and Papa to their Shabbos rest behind closed doors in the bedroom, and Rosie and I to play cards or reenact our favorite Bible stories. "This week you be Leah, I'll be Rachel." "No, you were Rachel last time, remember? I know—let's do Miriam watching Moshe and the Egyptian princess!" Or we would read aloud till dusky shadows filled the room, when we would climb into my bed and snuggle close beneath the covers whispering and giggling.

Lying next to Rosie, I began to sense my body in a new way. She was all lightness and delicacy; I was the solid, more substantial one. She made me conscious of the need to be gentle, so that I wouldn't bruise or crush or overwhelm her. Yet, next to Rosie, I did not feel imprisoned in my flesh as I did when I was with my brother. Rather, I felt complemented by her. She was the wings, I the muscle; together we would fly.

Rosie was more than a year older than I and slightly more developed. The angles of her shoulders, which I had come to know so well with my palms, were beginning to round, and her chest was no longer flat against mine. I was fascinated with the changes and wondered when they would start happening to me. I waited for Rosie to invite a closer inspection. I was very curious and desired to touch her nipples with my fingers. I wondered if grown-ups held each other like this, if a man would someday hold me and touch me as I was holding and wanted to touch Rosie. Would a man feel very different? I knew he would be bigger and rougher and probably hairy. He would feel prickly and make me itch from the hairiness. Yet it would be nice to snuggle up real small against a bigger body and feel warm and protected by him. I thought of the young men I had seen in the neighborhood—in the streets and in the stores, in shul, on their way to yeshiva; most of them were pale and skinny and wore glasses. I couldn't imagine wanting to hold any of them. I couldn't picture any man in Brooklyn being the least bit cuddly or warm or even nice to be near.

"Do you think it's like this when you're married?" I whispered.

"I don't know. I guess it's different," Rosie replied. "I think you get closer."

Our arms were wrapped around each other, our knees were touching, and one of her feet lay over my ankles.

"How could you get any closer?" I asked.

She didn't respond immediately.

"You know," she said. "We're just lying next to each other. But when you're married, your husband lies on top of you."

That seemed very uncomfortable to me. Why would

anyone want someone to lie on top of her? How would she breathe?

Rosie continued: "He not only lies on top of you, but he has to get inside you. Otherwise you can't have a baby."

I knew how babies were conceived. It had been explained in hygiene class, and we had been shown slides of the uterine canal and the ovaries with their eggs, and what happens when a sperm enters one of them. But it seemed so different hearing it from Rosie, lying close in the twilit shadows, her whispers moistening my neck and my cheeks. What she said bore no resemblance to the slides.

"Does it hurt?" I asked.

"I don't know, I've never done it." We giggled uncontrollably. We had to turn from each other and bury our faces in our pillows. I was trembling slightly and feeling giddy. It felt like Pesach, when Mama let me drink from the four cups of wine.

When we got control of ourselves, Rosie continued: "It's supposed to feel good. The man kisses the woman while he's doing it, so I guess that takes her mind off it."

Then we both lapsed into silence. I tried very hard to picture how it all happened. I didn't feel in the least sleepy as I usually did Shabbos afternoons. I could tell from the sound of her breathing that Rosie wasn't sleeping, either.

"Do you think we should try it?" I asked.

"We can't."

"Why not?"

"Two women can't do it together."

"Why not?"

"Don't you know biology? One of them needs a you-know-what."

I felt ashamed of my ignorance. Of course, I knew that the man had to use his you-know-what, but I thought maybe it didn't matter so much and we could do it without one.

After a while, she spoke again: "But I think we can try the kissing part. That would be okay."

I hesitated.

"What's the matter, don't you want to?" she asked.

"Of course I want to."

I was suddenly feeling very scared. I had kissed people before—my family, friends, Rosie, too. But this somehow seemed different. For one thing, it was secret. I had never kissed anyone in secret before. For another thing, I knew it would be a different kind of kiss. I'd seen kissing in the movies and on television, and it wasn't the same as the affection I exchanged with my family and my friends at school. I was sorry I had brought up the issue.

"Well?" she asked.

"All right," I said. "What do we do?"

"We just kiss, that's all."

"Who starts?"

"We both do, dumb-dumb."

I felt hurt. Suddenly I wanted to cry.

But then she slid close to me, so that one arm slipped

beneath my neck. We faced each other. She raised herself on one elbow, her hair brushed my cheek. It was soft and made me think of feathers and baby birds. Her skin had a smell I had never before noticed. It wasn't like the cologne you get out of a bottle. It was sharper—a sort of sweaty smell. Then it seemed as if the smell was coming from me; we were so close it was hard to tell. My heart was pounding. It's both our smells, I thought. We're doing it together. And then her lips were against mine, and I felt something wet flutter across them. I pressed my lips tight, because I thought maybe it was only the movie kind of kiss that was a sin, but if I kept my mouth closed, it would be all right. She kissed me hard. My teeth cut into my lips. It was uncomfortable to breathe. I wished it was over.

She drew her face away.

I ran my tongue over the inside of my lip. I tasted salt. I felt blood.

"Did you like it?" she asked.

I nodded yes.

"Do you love me?"

I thought it was a silly question. We were cousins; we were best friends. Of course I loved her. But I knew she was asking because in the movies they always asked that after they kissed or made love.

We both lay very still. Twilight had sifted from the room. It was night.

"Are you sorry?" she whispered.

"No," I lied. "Are you?"

"No."

Yellow bars of light appeared on the ceiling. Mrs. Feinblum across the alley had already bid farewell to the holy day. I wondered if everyone would be able to tell what Rosie and I had done. Would we be punished with loss of our friendship? Oh no, I couldn't bear that! I couldn't imagine Shabbos without Rosie. The yellow lights blurred. They swayed and danced on the ceiling. Warm tears trickled down my cheeks.

"Miriam . . ." she whispered.

"Yes?"

"You're not mad at me, are you?"

Oh no, a thousand times no! I wasn't mad. I didn't know why I was crying. I tried to hold back my sobs, but they came bursting out of me. And then we were both crying and holding each other.

"Shh—shhh . . . it's okay. Don't cry."

"I'm not angry, are you?"

"I love you. We're still friends, aren't we?"

"Forever."

"Let's never tell!"

"Of course not!"

"Then . . . it's all right. It's all right, then. . . ."

# CHAPTER
# 13

But later that winter, everything changed. Mama and Tante Sophie had another argument. It was right downstairs in the street where everyone could hear.

Tante shouted, "What makes you think you're so holy? You're not holy—you're superstitious—with all that medieval ritual!"

Mama spoke softly, but there was an edge to her voice which frightened me. I thought I detected hidden meaning in what she was saying. "I can no longer allow my Miriam to enter a Jewish home where the Law is not respected."

Had she somehow found out about Rosie and me? Did she blame Tante Sophie for our sin? Yet she did say, "Rosie will still be welcome in our house." I supposed this was so she could keep an eye on us.

Tante retorted, "You think you're better than everyone! I won't let my Rosie go to your house, either."

Upstairs, I pleaded with Mama. "What's the difference what Tante does? Rosie and I don't break the Law." My face grew very warm. I wondered if Mama understood why I was suddenly so flushed.

"Don't argue with me, Miriam. Believe me, this way is the lesser of two evils—"

What "evils" was she referring to? Why didn't she just come out and say that she knew about us? But then she continued: "They don't keep Shabbos in that house. There's no love of God or of His Torah. I don't want you exposed to that. You'll get it soon enough anyway when you grow up."

I felt relieved but confused. "What do you mean?" I demanded.

But she pursed her lips and nodded and said nothing more.

The image of Uncle Yitzrok with his hand on Mama's arm flashed through my mind. I sensed that it was more than disagreement about religion; Mama also wanted to separate our families for reasons of her own, having nothing to do with Rosie and me.

That's when my beloved Shabbos lost its spirit for me. I saw Rosie only at a distance in shul, for Mama made sure we sat well apart. After services, when we were all crowded in the vestibule, buttoning coats and wrapping scarves and wishing each other the customary "Good Shabbos" and "Shabbot Shalom," Mama made a point of extending a useless invitation to Rosie, useless because she knew, and so did Rosie and I, that it was forbidden for her to accept. Mama's smiling persistence angered me. I felt she was being dishonest, but I wasn't sure how. Mama, who taught me to kindle the Shabbos lights and to braid a challah and to be scrupulous in my knowledge and observance of all the minutiae of kashrut.

During the week, Rosie and I had little contact. We were in none of the same classes, and she stayed late every day to practice with the school orchestra or to study in the library, while I was expected to come directly home. We ran into each other occasionally in the corridor of the G.O. store. The first time, I threw my arms around her as we used to do whenever we met, even if we'd just seen each other the day before. But she backed away; an expression of fear or anger—I couldn't tell which—flitted across her face. I wondered if she, too, still worried about that Shabbos afternoon. I felt hurt, but I tried to cover it up.

"How's everything?" I asked.

"Fine," she replied.

We used to tell each other every detail of what had happened between our meetings. Now I felt so cut off from her I wanted to cry, but I held it in. "What's the matter?" I asked.

"Nothing." She seemed annoyed with my question. "I'm in a hurry, that's all. I just broke my shoelace, and I have to get a new one and get back upstairs to gym."

I knew she was lying, because the gym classes were all so crowded that it wouldn't matter how long she stayed out. Besides, she could always say there was a long line at the G.O. store, in case anyone asked. That's what I would do if she wanted to be with me. But she bought her laces and left.

It was the same whenever we met. She was always in a hurry. One by one, the angels that had danced between us folded their wings and fell to earth.

# 14

I'd always pictured my beginning high school as the start of a wonderful adventure. Rosie, one year ahead of me, would take me around and introduce me to all her friends. "I want you to meet my cousin Miriam. She's a lot of fun. You'll like her." And they would welcome me into their clique. Lunchtime, we would eat together, and after school we would go for ice cream, talking and laughing and making plans for good times on the weekend.

But with Rosie gone from me, high school seemed dreary and dull. I welcomed the difficulty of the new subjects and the workload because it kept me from thinking so much about my loneliness, though I couldn't stop feeling it.

One day, late in November, as I was leaving English class, Mrs. Hartman called me to her desk. When all the other pupils were gone, she put her hand on my shoulder.

"What's wrong, Miriam? You look as if something's bothering you."

Her gentleness made me want to cry.

"It's all right, Miriam, it's all right." Then she waited

for me to say something, but how could I tell her about Rosie and me? I couldn't tell anyone. No one must ever know what we had done together and why she had left me. So after I caught my breath I said, "I miss my brother."

"Has he gone somewhere?"

"He goes to yeshiva and he studies all the time and I hardly see him anymore."

As I thought about what I was saying, I started crying again. I really did miss him. Being with Rosie all the time had sort of covered it up, because I loved her, too—but it didn't change things.

Mrs. Hartman waited till I calmed down before she spoke again. "I think you need to be making some new friends. I know it's hard."

Then her voice lightened as she said, "Why don't you be in the winter pageant? I'm sure you'd be an excellent actress—and rehearsals are fun. It's a good way to make new friends."

In fifth grade I had had the lead in the class play— I loved the rehearsals because I could pretend I was someone else and no one could say anything mean to me, because we all had special lines that were in the script. And at the end, I took a bow all by myself and everyone applauded.

So I agreed, and Mrs. Hartman said she'd speak to the teacher in charge. The next morning she told me "it was all arranged" and that I should report to my first rehearsal at two o'clock. She wrote a note to my gym teacher to please excuse me.

I was all excited as I walked down the aisle of the auditorium to introduce myself to Mr. Manning.

"Oh yes, Miriam. Mrs. Hartman said she thought you'd be very good. . . ."

As he spoke to me, from somewhere in the left section, I heard, "Yoo-hoo! Skinny! You gonna join us?"

"She can't. She'd break the stage!"

Everyone laughed. It sounded like thunder. I tried to block them out.

Mr. Manning reached into his briefcase and handed me some pages. "You can play the farmer's wife, Miriam. It's a good part and we haven't cast it yet. We're about to work on that scene."

"Act One, Scene Three," he announced to the group. A few boys and girls filed into the aisle and up the steps to the platform. They were all holding typed white pages like mine.

"Go on, Miriam, this is your scene, too. Join them.'

The hooter was up there, leering at me. I hesitated. Then I climbed the steps, determined to enter into another life where no one could hurt me.

"Top of page eleven. Start where the farmer says, 'Who is it? Who's making such a commotion?' "

Francine giggled and poked Alan. "Go on, Alan, meet your new wife." Then everyone giggled as Alan cleared his voice and said, "My good wife, why don't you open the door?"

My line was next: "Yes, husband, I'm going. I'm going. Who is it?" I didn't know where to go, but I tried to imagine a door and went to open it.

"Very good, Miriam," Mr. Manning called. "Only a little more upstage—away from the audience." I moved and opened the door. Now I was face to face with the hooter. I held my breath; would he be nasty or follow the script?

"We're weary travelers who have come miles to spread the good news. May we come in? It's cold out there."

"Husband?"

"Yes, yes, let them enter."

"Sirs, what is your news?"

"A wonderful thing, good farmer. In a manger down the road a prince has been born. Look, sir, through your window. See that star shining brightly—"

My hands began trembling. I had gotten involved in a Christmas play. I knew Mama and Papa would forbid it. But even if they didn't find out, I felt it was wrong— probably sinful.

"Miriam, it's your line!"

I'd lost my place in the script.

"It's four lines down, where she says—"

I saw the words, but by then my hands had turned icy cold and I began to stammer.

Mr. Manning came to the foot of the stage. "What's the matter, Miriam? Don't you feel well?"

"I—I—it's just that—I—"

"What is it?"

"I—didn't know—what kind of play—I mean—I— I can't be in a Christmas play. I'm Jewish—my mama would forbid it. I didn't know. . . ."

"But Miriam, most of the other boys and girls are

Jewish too. That doesn't matter. It's only a play."

"I know. But I can't—"

Carol's voice piped up: "She's Jewish! She can't be in this play!"

"Her mama wouldn't allow it!" called another voice from the front row. Then everyone began laughing.

Mr. Manning spoke softly to me: "Are you sure, Miriam? Our spring play is about Passover. You can be in that one, too. Wouldn't that make it all right?"

I wanted to act in a play so much I was nearly in tears. But I knew it just wasn't right.

I shook my head. "No. I don't think so. Thank you. I have to go now—" and I ran up the aisle and out the rear door.

# CHAPTER
# 15

I used to watch Mama after she blessed the candles, the delicate, tapered flames gently swaying, casting a soft, mystical aura and filling the room with shalom. She would cover her face with her hands, concealing, even from me, her private conversation with God. In peace, in stillness, in rapt concentration, she would pour out her heart before her Creator. Occasionally, as she lowered her hands, I saw her lips still moving in prayer. How comforted I used to feel by Mama's prayer, knowing she was beseeching God on behalf of me and my brother and Papa and all Yisroel. But now, with the knowledge that she had shut out Rosie, deprived her of sharing our Shabbos, of eating at our table and singing zmirot with us, and perhaps even been responsible for Uncle's abandoning all of us, I could no longer believe Mama was truly praying for the good of all Yisroel and for peace among all people. And if she was not praying for blessings for us all, then why was she pretending? Was she imploring God only on her own and our immediate family's behalf? But this was not the way of Torah.

With the coming of spring, I resumed my Shabbos

afternoon strolls. Eagerly I made my way in and out of all the streets that Rosie and I used to frequent, expecting to meet her at every turn. I made long excursions to the park by the river. On warmer Shabbosim, we used to sit on a bench and watch the slow parade of passersby in their fine Sabbath dress, and listen to the swallows and the gulls, and whisper secrets that, even if spoken aloud, would have interested no one. Now, in late March, I watched alone, shoulders hunched against the stiff breeze blowing off the river. I wondered how Rosie felt when she thought about that Shabbos afternoon so long ago. I experienced a tenderness so profound and so private that I didn't dare share it— even with God. When thoughts of it intruded in my prayers, I simply prayed faster and faster, so the words would crowd out my feelings. Sometimes I felt as though I were being chased. But other times I let myself daydream, and then I wept with my desire.

A month of Shabbosim passed before I happened to meet Rosie. I was on my way to the river. She was with a group of classmates on line outside the movie theater. Our glances met, but she quickly averted her eyes. I wanted to call her, but she started to talk with the girl behind her, making it clear she did not wish to speak to me.

I kept my pace as I passed the movie theater, not wanting to betray my disappointment in front of everyone. As I waited for the traffic light, my vision blurred. Don't cry yet—not yet, I told myself. I ran the remaining few blocks, eager to be alone. There, by the river, in the presence of God, would I be able to pour out my heart. But it was a mild, breezy April afternoon, and the park was too crowded for that. There was no place for solitude except within my own heart. I kept picturing Rosie as she turned away from me on line, and I kept remembering how close we used to be.

For a long time after I lost Rosie, we still played together—in my imagination. Every Shabbos, after lunch, I retreated to my room to act all the parts in my favorite Bible tales. Then I read my books until I was too drowsy to stay awake, so that I wouldn't miss the real Rosie when I curled up in bed.

During the week, my fantasy cousin was always waiting for me to walk back and forth to school. Sometimes she sat beside me in class when I finished my work ahead of the others and had nothing to do; or during outdoor gym, when everyone was talking and laughing and I felt left out, she would join me at the far end of the school-yard. We didn't talk then, because someone might see and think I was "crazy." She just stayed with me.

No one knew my secret. It was nice having Rosie this way—we never argued; she was always there when I wanted her. But it frightened me, too, because I suspected there was probably something "not right" in my having an invisible friend. So I promised myself that, by my next birthday, I would give her up. But I couldn't. The thought of spending the whole day without her was unbearable. I tried reading a lot so I wouldn't miss her so much, but my mind kept wandering.

"Why are you always moping around the house?"

Papa demanded. He never asked as though he wanted to hear what I had to say, but rather as though he was commanding me to change. This made me so angry I wanted to scream or throw things, but I knew that would only make things worse. So I spent as little time as possible at home. Most afternoons, I went to the library to read articles on psychology and find out whether or not I was crazy. But I couldn't find the answer. So I decided to be safe and demote Rosie to the status of pen pal. I broke the news to her one afternoon on the way home from the library.

"It's you who stopped being friends in the first place," I told her. "So I can't keep being friends with you. But I'll write to you, anyway."

She cried and begged me to change my mind. I didn't think I'd ever see her cry for me. I was surprised at how happy it made me feel to cause her pain. I would not relent. I made up my mind to try talking more to my classmates during homeroom and free time and to think about other things walking to and from school, knowing that I could write to Rosie at night in the privacy of my room. And I promised myself that even this would stop soon, and it did. I started doing service in school for Mrs. Hartman. It was the second time I had her for English. She loved the compositions I did for class, and I soon decided it would be more fun to write stories I could read aloud to everyone than to keep writing letters to a Rosie who would never read them.

The audience I loved best was Moshele. He didn't

have much time for me, as he spent every afternoon in yeshiva or shul preparing for his bar mitzvah, which was less than one year off. But when he did listen, he would close his eyes, and I knew he was picturing everything I was describing. Once or twice, when the story was particularly sad, he even started to cry, which made me very happy. He never asked why I wrote such sad stories; he never complained that I didn't smile enough. We didn't say much when we were together; I read and he listened. That was all. But I knew he loved me.

As his bar mitzvah approached, he often ate supper at the home of one of the older boys who was learning with him. I missed him. Even though he rarely spoke at the table, I used to feel comforted by his presence. When Mama and Papa raised their voices, Moshe and I would exchange a quick glance, which was enough to assure me that I wasn't alone.

These days, Moshe's bar mitzvah was the only concern around the house. We spent entire afternoons and evenings shopping for the right clothes for the big day. Usually Mama made her dresses and mine, too, but for the bar mitzvah she wanted a "professional job." The bar mitzvah was going to be one of the biggest events the shul ever had. Moshe already had a reputation for being a "Talmud chochem," a Torah scholar, and everyone in the neighborhood was coming to hear his speech.

Now that he would become a "son of the Commandments," I would no longer be hearing him daven in his room in the mornings; I'd no longer be able to time my own prayers so that they might be joined to his. For Moshe would be leaving very early to daven with a minyan in shul. He would take his place in a congregation of men, and all together they would recite, "Blessed art Thou, Lord our God, King of the Universe, for not making me a woman." Then most of them would hurry home to eat the breakfast their wives or mothers cooked for them. Mama and the other women seemed to take for granted that this was as it should be.

"I don't see why the women have to sit in the balcony in shul," I said to her.

"What's the matter, you never minded before."

"Well, I mind now."

"So go complain to the rabbi."

Trying to talk about my feelings with Mama only made me angrier.

# CHAPTER
# 16

A week before the bar mitzvah, Papa started bringing things home from the store. We had ordered a special catered dinner for relatives and friends in a hall at night, and we were making an elaborate kiddush, a blessing with lots of wine and food, for everyone in the shul after morning services. All afternoon, we would be having open house.

Moshe was home with me the afternoon the Partner came to see us. When the doorbell rang, I thought that Mama had forgotten her key. At first, I didn't recognize the figure in the dim-lit hallway, draped in a long overcoat with earmuffs underneath his hat. I was frightened. I knew I shouldn't have opened the door without asking who it was.

I was about to slam it when he asked, "May I come in?" and I recognized Mr. Samuel.

"Mama isn't home now."

"May I wait inside? It's drafty in the hall."

I didn't like having him in the house. He gave me the creeps with his half-toothless leer and his singsong voice. I had taken pains to avoid the store as much as possible ever since the Candy Incident. But I couldn't be rude to him, so I stepped aside so he could enter. He sat in a chair at the kitchen table without removing his coat or his earmuffs or his hat. He gazed around the room, taking in everything.

"Don't let me keep you." He smiled as though to put me at my ease. But it only made me more nervous, because Mama wasn't here and Mr. Samuel had no business being here either. I tried to be hospitable.

"Would you like a cup of tea?" Mama offered "a glassele tea" to everyone, even if they only came to borrow an onion.

"Thank you, no." He gestured with his hand. After a while he asked, "Where's the bar mitzvah boy?"

"In his room. Studying."

I wondered what he wanted with my brother. Would he try to spoil his bar mitzvah to avenge himself for the candy?

"May I wish him a mazel tov?"

I should have told him Moshe couldn't be disturbed. But instead I said, "I'll go get him." I remained glued to Moshe's side as he came to the doorway.

The Partner lunged toward him with his arm extended. "Mazel tov! Mazel tov! Such a fine bar mitzvah boy! Mazel tov!" Moshe accepted his handshake limply.

"Are you all ready for the big day? I bet you'll make your mama and papa so proud—they're already so proud of you. Such a gantse megillah they're making for your bar mitzvah—" Mr. Samuel ran on excitedly. Moshe stared at him in silence. I tried to think of some way to cut in and suggest he come back another time if he wanted to speak with Mama. Then, without pausing, the Partner stood tall and gestured toward the boxes of cookies stacked on the open pantry shelves and on top of the refrigerator.

"Your papa's been preparing over a week already," he said. "For ten days, the cookies have been disappearing. And jars of horseradish. And, two days ago, the herrings and the lox and the whitefish. They're making a real fancy megillah—a meat affair. For your sister, it was just dairy." He turned toward me. "I remember your bas mitzvah, Miriam. It was a nice spread, but only dairy. Your papa walked home with half the store. But what could I say? We were partners. But then I bought him out! We're not partners anymore. He works for me now!" He began to shriek. "A worker—an employee—that's all your papa is! And he still has the chutzpah to keep taking! And nothing but the best, too. For little Moshele's bar mitzvah—nothing but the best!" He paused to wipe the thin line of spittle which had formed around the corners of his mouth.

"And do you know how I know it's a meat affair?" His voice trailed up hills and down valleys, as it did when I was a little girl and he used to tell me things. "I know because only the pareve is disappearing this time. The cheeses and the cream—all the dairy he's not touching. So I said to myself, 'They're having the sit-down dinner catered—a meat affair.'"

Moshe and I exchanged glances. I felt he was saying, "Make this man leave, Sissa! Why do you let him stay?" But I couldn't think of anything to say which wouldn't sound rude. Mama always taught me to respect a grown-up, even if I didn't agree with him or like what he was saying. I wanted to say something in Papa's defense, but I couldn't think of a thing. Mama and Papa never discussed "store business" in front of us. I felt as though we were being violated, all of us together, and I was powerless to prevent it. Finally, I found the voice to say, "I don't know when Mama will be home. Maybe you should come back—"

"Yes—yes! I was just going." His long black coatsleeves flapped like the wings of a vulture as he pumped Moshe's hand again. "Mazel tov—mazel tov!" And he backed toward the door.

"Tell your mama I was here." Then, still smiling, he paused and seemed to hover over the theshold before he finally turned and left. Moshe looked at me accusingly. I realized that Mr. Samuel had not come to speak to Mama but to pour his venom into our ears—and I had let him.

There was no need to tell Mama anything. She and Papa came in a moment later. They must have met Mr. Samuel in the hall or on the stairs. They were both pale. Mama's lips were pursed. Papa's skin seemed too loose on him; his cheeks sagged, and pouches hung beneath his eyes. Mama helped him off with his coat and took his scarf and handed them to me to put in the closet. Moshe went to Mama and took her coat and hat. Papa leaned on the back of a chair for support. Mama stood protectively by his side. His shoulders were slightly stooped, and his body seemed concave, as though he had lost fifty pounds since morning. I became frightened. In the moment we stood facing one another, I felt us draw together. All the irritations and minor disagreements that I had with Mama and Papa were suddenly swept away. I wanted them to know I would stand by them no matter what. I wanted us all to put our arms around one another and to give one another strength. Together we would support Papa. Suddenly I knew what Mama had meant by a "family matter." These were the things I was never to speak of.

Mama's gaze held us motionless. I felt as though she was drawing us into an everlasting covenant. Then she spoke so softly we nearly had to stop breathing in order to hear.

"Your papa did nothing wrong. Everything he does is for your sake. For all of our sakes. He loves us all too much. That's his trouble. There's not a selfish, greedy bone in his body." She concluded with "Go to your room."

No one ate dinner that night. No one spoke, no one moved. It was as though someone had died.

I lay down on my bed on top of the covers. I didn't want to sleep, only to think—not even to think, but to be alone and still. Through the closed door, I felt their silence in the kitchen. I pictured them frozen, just as they were when Mama sent us to our room. I felt Moshe's stillness on the other side of the partition. For once, he wasn't davening aloud or chanting. There were no pages rustling; his chair didn't creak. I knew he must be lying down, too, trying to understand what had happened in the light of Torah.

The Partner's face hung suspended in the twilight. I wondered if Moshe saw it, too. He was saying, "For you—just dairy. But for Moshe, a gantse megillah—a meat affair!" It was funny how I didn't get angry at Mama and Papa as I always did when they favored Moshe. Instead, I had wanted to defend them—to say, "What's it to you?" And close my ears and turn the Partner away.

It grew dark. I wondered how late it was. My stomach was churning, but I couldn't tell whether from hunger or nausea. It felt strange, not knowing whether it was dinnertime or midnight.

Mama and Mr. Samuel were arguing. Mr. Samuel said, "Everything disappears—the cookies, the herrings, your brother-in-law. Even the children—"

And Mama said, "You leave them out of this!"

Then Mr. Samuel laughed, and the rest of his teeth fell out. When that happened, I knew he was truly evil and that even the Shechina would not be able to redeem him. Uncle Yitzrok had said that God leads man in the way that he wants to go. I wondered which way I would go.

# CHAPTER
# 17

The floorboards creaked. I heard a bureau drawer open, then more creaking. Had I been dreaming? Moshe was tiptoeing on his side of the room. What was he doing? Then the chiffon curtain rustled as he brushed by.

I whispered, "Moshe?"

I could feel him holding his breath. He was so still I began to doubt I'd heard him in the first place. Maybe that was part of my dream, too.

"Where are you going?"

"Shhhhhh!"

I pulled the curtain aside. He was carrying a towel neatly rolled under his arm.

"Go to sleep," he said, like a father to a child.

"Where are you going?"

"Somewhere. I can't tell you."

"But it's the middle of the night."

"Shh—go back to sleep. You'll wake Mama and Papa."

"First tell me where you're going!"

"I can't."

I sat up. "Then I won't let you go."

A look of despair crossed his face. "Please, I gotta

104

go somewhere. It's very important. I'll tell you later—when I come back."

"Tell me now."

He didn't respond. I could tell he was trying to decide how far he could trust me. Then he came very close and whispered, "I'm going to the mikvah."

"The mikvah? But that's for women!"

"It's for anyone who needs to be purified."

"It's the middle of the night. The mikvah's not open."

"It doesn't have to be a regular mikvah in a house. As long as it's 'living waters.' I'm going to the river."

"You can't—not in the middle of the night. It's February. You can't go to the river!"

"I have to. I've been defiled."

I thought of the Candy Incident so long ago. Was he referring to that? Or to Papa and the store, or to Uncle Yitzrok and Mama? I wondered if immersion in the "living waters" would cleanse me, too.

"Let me come with you."

"You can't. I have to undress."

"I won't look."

"No."

I knew that once my brother decided something he wouldn't budge. But I pursued it anyway. If only I could detain him long enough, it would get light, and then we could both go to the regular mikvah.

"You weren't responsible," I said. "You were only five years old when you did it."

He looked surprised. "Did what? What are you talking about?"

"The candy," I said. "It wasn't your fault. Papa led us to believe—"

"Don't talk about Papa! I won't listen. My sin is worse. It's double. I listened to gossip—and I felt disrespect toward Papa in my heart."

I was confused. How could he erase the stealing from his mind, yet blame himself for something so trivial as listening to Mr. Samuel?

"It wasn't your fault," I repeated.

"Then whose fault is it?" he demanded. "Torah teaches that the one who listens to gossip is as guilty as the one who speaks it. How can I go up to the Torah on Shabbos? How can I be bar mitzvah? I'm defiled. I've sinned. I'll defile the Torah. I have to cleanse myself."

I felt it was *my* sin for which he was atoning. I should have sent Mr. Samuel away.

He whispered, "I'll come right back. Don't tell Mama I'm going."

I was of two minds. If Moshe could atone for us both, why not let him? I didn't really feel like going out in the bitter cold anyway.

"Promise?" he asked.

"I promise."

He sighed. "Thanks, Sissa."

I listened for his footsteps in the kitchen and for the door to open and close behind him. But he didn't make a sound. I had an eerie image of him floating through the walls to do God's bidding.

As soon as he left, I was sorry I'd promised. I thought I knew the place by the river where he would go. There was a small grove of trees between the path and the water's edge where we all used to go on Shabbos afternoons in summer a very long time ago—the four of us and Uncle Yitzrok, Tante Sophie, and Rosie. I decided to dress quickly and go after Moshe.

The night air was razor sharp. There was no wind, but the sheer cold stung my cheeks and my thighs, which were bare beneath my coat and skirt. I'd forgotten my gloves, so I kept my hands in my pockets as I half walked, half ran through the deserted streets. I wanted to call out to Moshe. Everything was so icy still I knew my voice would carry, but I was afraid of waking the neighbors. I felt I was doing something wild and adventurous. Above, a crescent moon hung frozen in the sky. It reminded me of the silver cup we used to pour the water for the ritual blessing every time we ate bread. It made me feel safe.

I was grateful for the crunching of the gravel underfoot when I reached the river path. It would frighten off any unfriendly spirits that might be lurking behind the trees or in the brambles. I paused to listen. Silence. Then the soft, rhythmic lapping of the water, as though it were breathing. I continued on tiptoe, pausing every few steps to listen for some sound from Moshe. And then it came. A sharp, hacking cough, like a tiny hammer on a block of wood.

"Moshele!" I called.

The cough stopped suddenly—then started again, muffled. I followed the sound. He was seated on a clump of earth in his undershorts, untying his shoes, a bath towel wrapped around his shoulders. His frailty frightened me.

"Moshe, you'll get sick! Get dressed!"

"I t-told you not to come. Go away! Please," he begged. "J-just walk away for f-five minutes so I can finish g-getting undressed and immerse. Then I'll c-c-come home with you."

There was no arguing with Moshe. So I agreed to wait on the other side of the bushes. I hopped from one foot to the other trying to keep warm. I wished I had argued with him harder while we were still in the house. I should have woken Mama and Papa and not have worried that Moshe would have been mad at me. I prayed to God to keep my brother safe and not let him get sick. I kept repeating my prayer as I hopped from foot to foot, so I couldn't think of anything else, and pretty soon it was all over. Moshe called to me. He was dressed in his shirt and trousers and trembling violently. I threw his coat over his shoulders as he sat to tie his shoelaces. Ice crystals clung to his wet hair. I used the towel to rub his scalp. He didn't object. He stood and thrust his arms through his sleeves. I never saw a human being shake as much as he was shaking. He put his cap on, and I pulled up his collar and took off my scarf and wrapped it around him. He slipped his hand into mine as he used to when we were very little—and we ran all the way home.

I wondered whether he felt purified and closer to God now. But he was shivering and chattering so hard, even after we got upstairs, that I could only concentrate

on ways to make him warm. I heated a glassful of hon-
eyed lemonade and set it on his night table so he could
drink it when he came out of the bathroom. Then I
crawled into bed. I kept telling myself, "As long as he
did a mitzvah, he won't get sick. Nothing bad can happen to him." I chanted it softly to the traditional can-
tilations Moshe used when he learned Torah. I lay back
on my pillow chanting and closed my eyes and felt great
waves of weariness wash over me.

# CHAPTER
# 18

Sunlight was streaming into the room. It seemed much later than seven o'clock. I knew I'd overslept. I rubbed my eyes and sat up. How come Mama hadn't woken me? Wasn't it a schoolday? I felt disoriented. The events of the night before floated through my mind . . . Moshe . . . the river . . . Mr. Samuel . . . Papa . . . were they real or had I imagined them? "Every day something disappears . . . the cookies, a herring . . . your brother . . ." I jumped out of bed and peeked around the partition. Moshe was sleeping peacefully, his head inclined toward the vaporizer. His face seemed to blend into the pillowcase. But he looked happy. I collected my clothes and tiptoed to the bathroom to dress. The clock from the bank chimed ten times. I had missed English and American History.

I listened outside the big bedroom, but it was very still. I knew they were both inside—that Papa hadn't gone to work. How would he be able to go into the store and face Mr. Samuel? Would he return all those boxes of cookies and the smoked fish? Would he apologize? Would Mr. Samuel shame him even more?

As I emerged from the bathroom, Mama met me.

Her eyes were puffy and her skin had the texture of chalk dust.

"Don't wake your papa or your brother," she whispered. "They need their sleep. Your brother was up at five o'clock. He couldn't catch his breath. I thought he was having an attack. He caught a chill. But you slept right through it."

I felt accused and angry. I thought of telling Mama how I'd run through the streets in the cold to keep Moshe safe and well, but it all seemed so unreal now.

"When you're ready to leave, tap on the door. Softly. I'll give you a late note for school." And she disappeared into her room.

I tiptoed into the kitchen. My stomach was grinding. It felt like an empty hole inside me. I wondered how much it would take to fill it up. I wanted company. I wanted my brother. I wanted to take care of him, to make breakfast for the two of us. I put the juice and date-nut bread and cereal and milk on the table and set two places. But no one came.

It felt strange to be leaving the house with everyone else still home. Early morning was usually a busy time. Papa left first, then Moshe. Mama was bustling around the stove the whole time. There was conversation, movement, clatter. But today the stillness was eerie. I wondered whether anyone would be out of bed, or whether it would still feel like a morgue when I came home. I knew Mama would keep Moshe in bed the rest of the week. With his bar mitzvah on Saturday, we couldn't take chances. She would phone the yeshiva, and Yussele and some of the other boys would visit in the afternoon to learn with him.

It was a relief to get out of the house, though I didn't really want to go to school. The only time the other kids noticed me in a good way was when I read my stories or compositions aloud in English. I liked doing service for Mrs. Hartman during my study periods. We would sit alone in the classroom, she at her desk and me at mine, and she would let me mark the spelling and the short answers from all her classes. Sometimes we would hardly say a word, but I knew she understood my feelings by the way she smiled when our eyes met and the way she'd put her hand on my shoulder and say, "Thank you, Miriam. You're a big help to me," when the change bell rang. But I'd already missed English, and I had no study period today. So I'd have to plod through the hours till I could run home to see how Moshele was doing and, if I was lucky, maybe start writing a story I could read in class later in the week.

# CHAPTER
# 19

Shul was packed on Shabbos. Upstairs, where Mama and I sat side by side in the first row, a dozen women squeezed onto each bench meant for nine. Downstairs, Moshe, sallow and very serious, enthroned on the seat of honor facing the bimah, quietly received the mazel tovs and good wishes heaped upon him. The men all looked alike from behind in their white prayer shawls and their brimmed hats and yarmulkes. I knew Papa was in the first row, but I scanned the congregation for Uncle Yitzrok. I was sure he'd return for Moshe's bar mitzvah. My eye fixed on a tall, thin figure in the third row, one of the few already immersed in prayer. As he swayed and gently rocked to the rhythm of his prayers, I could picture Uncle's large dark eyes concealing the Mysteries of the Universe, their lids about to close as he received divine inspiration for a parable. The women's section was still buzzing with conversation. Arms and faces and bosoms of all shapes and sizes bobbed and reached and pressed themselves against Mama and me, tearful smiles and mazel tovs abounding. Tante and Rosie weren't there yet. They would, as usual, arrive at the last minute, probably just as Moshe was being called to the Torah. The men's section was settling down. From above, it resembled an undulating sea of white. Sometimes I let its hypnotic effect wash over me—but this morning I was too excited and too distracted by everyone around me. I reached for a prayer book and held it open on my lap. Moshe was rapt in concentration, as though none of us existed. I half expected him to rise effortlessly from the chair and float over the entire congregation, beseeching God on behalf of us all. I was sure God had set aside everything to listen to Moshele's speech, though He had probably never noticed mine. I thought, A big bar mitzvah in shul with a sit-down meat reception is certainly more important than a little dairy affair at home. I felt angry, yet proud of my brother at the same time.

We were up to the longest prayer of all, the standing Silent Devotion. A hush descended as we all took three steps back and three forward to enter into the Presence of God. I glanced at Mama. Would she be willing to forget her differences with Tante Sophie so Rosie and I might resume our friendship? A joyous occasion is supposed to erase bad feelings. But would it?

The Ark was opened, the Holy Scrolls removed. We leaned forward and watched as they were paraded around the men's section to be kissed. Then the first scroll was brought to the bimah, its velvet casing and silver ornaments removed. Moshe was summoned. Mama and I pressed against the railing to catch every syllable. The rabbi called Papa to take his place beside Moshe and recite the first blessing. Papa's skin was ashen, with deep shadows in the hollows of his cheeks and under his eyes. The rabbis and the cantor towered over him. His new suit, which was tailored to order just a few weeks ago, bagged in the trousers. His prayer shawl dangled forlornly from his shoulders. Papa was inaudible. We all chanted the response, then the cantor read and Moshe was called. His voice was clarion. "Blessed be the Lord who is blessed." We responded: "Blessed be the Lord who is blessed forever and ever." He continued: "Blessed art Thou, Lord our God, King of the Universe, who has chosen us from amongst all peoples and given us Thy Torah. . . ."

Mama was weeping quietly. I took her hand and pressed it, but she seemed not to notice. The congregation was still. Moshe's voice, unfaltering, floated up from the bimah. It filled the shul with sweetness. When he finished, the congregation burst into a spontaneous and unprecedented applause. Mama wept loudly. Three or four nearby women, also weeping, threw their arms around her. There were loud whispers of "Mazel tov—ken-eine ha'ra! Mazel tov! He should live till a hundred and twenty!" Mama's hair, which she had spent half an hour arranging and pinning in place, was tousled—her lipstick was smeared, and on her cheeks were imprinted the lip marks of the other women. But her eyes shone and she looked very happy. Moshe had brought her honor. I wondered if I would ever be able to do the same for her. I glanced around in the commotion to see where Tante and Rosie were sitting. Toward the rear, near the door, Tante, in a bright turquoise dress, leaned forward in her place, nodding approvingly. She waved when our eyes met. I smiled back and mouthed, "Where's Rosie?" But she didn't understand. She smiled again and nodded. "Mazel tov! Mazel tov!" The rabbi paused for the congregation to collect itself before continuing with the worshipping. But the women's section did not calm down until Moshe stood at the bimah once again to deliver his d'var Torah. The subject of his talk was how God had hardened Pharaoh's heart, which he interpreted to mean that God leads man in the direction that he wants to go. My brother's direction was obvious—he would serve God. But I wondered which way I would choose and whether I would receive divine aid. There was a hush as the rabbi pronounced the benediction. Then the prayer service resumed. I became preoccupied with thinking about Rosie. As soon as the final hymn was sung, I edged my way toward Tante.

"Where's Rosie?"

She smiled apologetically and gave me a big hug and a resounding kiss on my cheek. "Your brother was wonderful!" she crooned. "Wonderful!" Then she leaned over to whisper in my ear. "Rosie has her period. She doesn't feel well. She said to tell you she's sorry."

I turned away from her so she wouldn't see my tears. I didn't believe Tante's excuse.

Everyone was crowding around Moshe and Mama and Papa, so they didn't notice me slipping off to the ladies' room to cry. I felt ashamed because I was unable to put aside my own concerns and enter into the communal joy of my brother's bar mitzvah. Uncle Yitzrok was always full of stories about the miracles that occur when the congregation of Israel rejoices together on religious occasions. I wondered what he would think of me. "God is found in joy and laughter and not in weeping and mourning," he used to say. "Wine maketh glad the heart." I wondered if he had found God since he had left and if he would tell us about it later. I rinsed my face with cold water and went to join the others and look for him.

They were all milling around the smorgasbord eating and talking. Now that I could see their faces, none of them looked like Uncle. The man I had mistaken for him from the rear was a young yeshiva student. I wondered if Moshe had seen Uncle, but there was no chance to ask because his teachers and friends surrounded him. So I wove in and out among the guests, looking for the right beard and hat and listening for the familiar "Aha!"

By the end table, where the smoked fishes were, stood Papa, laughing and flushed. He had one arm around Mama's shoulders, and with the other he clutched the edge of the table. Mama's brows were knit. They stood by the lox as though they expected Mr. Samuel to appear momentarily to snatch it away. I thought it strange how the people who weren't present seemed more real than those who were. Though I knew most of the guests by name, we had never spoken more than "Good Shabbos. How are you?" They were mostly grown-ups who knew who they were and what they wanted and how to get it. When would I be like that, I wondered. Even Moshe's friends, who were mostly younger than I, had decided their paths. I knew I didn't want to be like Mama, always watching out for Papa and Moshe and me. I wanted more. Yet all these other ladies were married and "were fruitful and multiplied," and they seemed happy. I didn't think I would mind being married if he was cute and not just studious. And if I could travel and write books and do wonderful things instead of diaper babies. But no man would want a wife who didn't give him children. "Being fruitful" was a commandment. I watched Moshe's friends. In a few years they would all look alike. Every one of them was already pale and round-shouldered from constant study. The older ones had scrubby whiskers and sideburns, and the younger would as soon as they were able. I was sure they all talked alike and thought alike and acted alike. And I imagined they would probably make love alike. Always proper, always according to Law. I wondered which ones Mama would invite home to meet me in the coming year or two. I wouldn't mind the one I had mistaken for Uncle Yitzrok. Perhaps he liked to sing and tell stories, too. I wished Moshe would introduce me. I was too shy to approach on my own. But Moshe seemed oblivious to my existence. So I pretended not to notice them, and I wandered around feeling like a shadow in a roomful of people. I was glad when everyone had done eating and talking, and started going for their coats.

People streamed into our house all afternoon. But not Rosie and not Uncle Yitzrok. Papa got very drunk and started singing loudly. Mama made him lie down in the bedroom, where everyone had put their coats. I wondered whether he was drunk with joy over my brother or drunk with shame and fear that Mr. Samuel might show up. When I caught Moshe alone on his way to the bathroom, I asked, "Do you think Uncle Yitzrok will come?" Moshe's face darkened; for the first time, I sensed bitterness in him. "No," he said. I was sorry I had asked. I tried to mend my mistake with a false note of hope. "Maybe he's just late. Maybe he'll come for the dinner." "I don't think so," Moshe replied. "Do you think he forgot?" Moshe shrugged. He seemed on the verge of tears. I hugged him. He allowed himself to be comforted for a moment, and then, as though remembering the impropriety of it, he pulled away.

After that, whenever I thought of Uncle, I saw the hurt on Moshe's face, and I grew angry.

# CHAPTER
# 20

A few nights after the bar mitzvah, I was awakened by gasping and wheezing. I peeked around the partition. Propped on four pillows, Moshe was struggling to breathe. Every now and then one of his arms would flail out as though he was fighting for air. His skin had a slight bluish tinge, so that he resembled pictures I'd seen of the dying in concentration camps. I ran to wake Mama.

"Quick—run the hot water in the tub—steam up the bathroom!" she ordered, fumbling to get out of bed.

The water was scarcely warm, so I filled the kettle and the big pots and set them going on the stove. Mama carried Moshe into the kitchen wrapped in his blanket, whistling and whooshing and wheezing. I drew two chairs together and went for a pillow and his spray medicine so he could rest more comfortably. All the while, he was becoming bluer. I arranged the pillow beneath his head while Mama phoned the doctor.

"No! It can't wait till morning!" she shouted into the receiver. "He can't breathe now! You gotta come now!" Then she quieted down, listening, murmuring, "Yes . . . Yes, Doctor . . . Yes, the emergency room . . . Yes

. . . You'll be there . . . All right, Doctor, yes. Thank you, Doctor . . ." And she hung up.

We had always avoided hospitals, even with Moshe's frequent crises. Once or twice, when the doctor had recommended we take him, Mama had stood adamant. "Nonsense! The hospital will make him worse. We take care of him at home." And she always did. I knew Mama had a dread of hospitals because she had had a baby sister who died in one. She used to tell us, "Stay away from the hospital, whatever you do! Mama took Ruthie, and the nurses were so careless, they left her in a draft. She was only two years old and she died. She'd be alive today if we didn't let them put her in the hospital."

There was a sense of security in knowing that, whatever the difficulty, Mama could handle it for us at home. So now, when she acquiesced to the doctor's order, I knew the situation was very serious. I knelt by Moshe's side and placed my hand on his forehead. I drew close, concentrating my thoughts on him. "Come on, Moshe, get better! Start breathing good." But I knew this was futile. Then I thought of psalms and prayers, but the only line that came to mind was, "Yea, though I walk through the valley of the shadow of death . . ." and I didn't want to say that, or even to think it. Then I remembered one of the rabbis saying that the shortest prayer on record was the one Moshe made for Miriam when she developed leprosy. He said, "Dear God, make her well." So I repeated, "Dear God, make him well." I said it over and over till it crowded out my feelings of helplessness and Mama and Papa emerged from their room ready to take him. They bundled him up in his coat and scarf and hat and wrapped him in three blankets till he no longer resembled a child in Papa's arms but some old rolled-up rug.

I wanted to go along, but Mama said, "There's nothing you can do, you'll only be in the way. Go back to sleep. If we need you, we'll telephone." I was always in the way where Moshe was concerned. I was either making too much noise or spreading germs or creating a draft or being a bad influence on him so that they needed to separate us.

I sat up in bed trying to read, determined not to allow myself to doze until I knew for sure that everything was all right. But I kept wandering from the book every few lines, trying to imagine what it must feel like not to be able to breathe. Finally, I just lay back on my pillow and closed my eyes. "Please, God, make him well."

"Your brother has double pneumonia," Mama announced when she woke me in the morning. Her eyes were red, her face drawn; I knew she hadn't been to sleep all night. She looked dry and wrinkled, like an old plant someone forgot to water; her voice rasped like dead autumn leaves blown by the wind, scratching and scraping and clicking along the pavement. Mama's grief alarmed me. Pneumonia, I'd heard of, but what was a double pneumonia? "What does it mean?"

"It means that Moshe's a very sick little boy. He's staying in the hospital for a few days." Tears welled in her eyes; she tried to squeeze them back, but they came streaming down her cheeks. I got out of bed and tried to put my arms around her as she used to do for me when I would cry. But she brushed me aside.

"You'll be late for school," she said. "Go get dressed. Visiting hours are from three to nine." Then she left my room. I could tell she was still crying; I heard it in her voice. I felt so helpless because I could do nothing to comfort her. She seemed to be saying, "I don't need your help. I don't need anyone." And now she had gone into the kitchen to fix my breakfast, as though, even at a time like this, she couldn't trust me to take care of myself. I peeked around the partition—maybe, just maybe, it was all in my imagination; I had just been dreaming. But his bed was empty.

All day in school, I kept thinking about Moshele in the hospital surrounded by strangers poking him and sticking him with needles and maybe being careless so that he'd get worse and die. Finally, it was dismissal time. As I waited by the bus stop, I kept watching for Rosie, hoping she would see me there and stop to inquire.

"I'll come with you," she would say. "It's a terrible place! You mustn't go all by yourself."

But she didn't pass that way. In front of me were some seniors, pushing each other and joking loudly in language I'd been taught never, never to repeat—or even to listen to. In back of me was my gym teacher and a bunch of younger pupils I'd seen around but didn't know. I was trying to devise a plan in my mind for checking up on the nurses to see they weren't careless with Moshe. What would happen if he couldn't breathe during the night and no one was around to take care of him? I was thinking about all these things as I got off the bus. I had hoped someone—anyone—my gym teacher or the bus driver—would ask me why I was going to the hospital. I had to tell someone—he's my only brother, and he's very sick! I had to share my anxiety. He has double pneumonia and they're keeping him in the hospital! I had felt so empty when I'd peeked around the partition in the morning and he wasn't there.

I turned the corner and faced the large gray stone façade of the hospital. The walls were checkered with row on row of small rectangular windows, behind each of which, I imagined, was some anonymous sick person. I couldn't understand how so many people could be suffering at one time. Where did they all come from? How many different sorts of sicknesses could people have? I wondered if each of the patients had a family who came to visit and friends who sent get-well cards and phoned and brought presents. It occurred to me that Moshe's schoolmates were probably not the type to send cards. I decided to buy him a nice one with colorful flowers and a poem inside and mail it to him. Moshe never received mail. He'd enjoy it.

I followed the broad, circular walkway to the main entrance. The lobby was bustling and warm; Muzak played softly. There were maroon carpets and puffy orange-brown sofas teeming with bulkily clad women and stony-faced men and babies and children, clutching tattered dolls and torn storybooks, climbing over each other and crying. Men and women hurried by; the revolving door was in constant motion. There was black grief and Oriental grief and Spanish grief and Jewish grief, and it was all the same.

I followed the yellow arrows to the elevators in the east wing. Once I left the main lobby, the feeling I had of warmth and of community evaporated. The corridor was long, the walls bare except for ominous directions pointing the way to RADIOLOGY or CHEMOTHERAPY or OUTPATIENT DIALYSIS, as though people were being classified by their particular kinds of suffering. You—turn right, the work camp! You—left, the crematorium— You—get on the table under the machine— You—into this room so we can drain your blood! Were these the decisions that God made on Yom Kippur when He inscribed the fate of every human being in His Book? Was that when Moshe's double pneumonia was mandated? Did God already know who would live and who would die? Did He inscribe a different kind of fate for those like my brother who were totally pious and observed all the commandments?

The elevator numbers lit up at each floor. When the doors slid open, I found myself opposite a counter laden with potted plants and large bouquets of flowers in green glass vases. Nurses and young doctors, their stethoscopes dangling like shiny silver ornaments around their necks, hurried down the long fluorescent corridor, pausing by some rooms, entering others, coming, going.

A nurse approached me. "Can I help you?"

I told her Moshe was my brother.

"Follow the corridor through the door at the end where it says ISOLATION—AUTHORIZED PERSONS ONLY. Go through that door, he's the second room on your right. But wait—" She went behind the counter and brought out a white face mask with strings attached, the kind the doctors wore on TV.

"Better let me help you with this," she said. "You have to wear it the whole time so you don't catch anything. Everyone on that side of the door is contagious."

As I held the mask over my nose and mouth, and I felt her fingers at the back of my head, catching my hair once or twice as she tied the strings, I remembered the kerchief Mama used to tie over my face whenever she led me in to see the baby. For an instant, I experienced the panic of not being able to breathe and the impulse to rip off the cloth before I suffocated. The first few times Mama tied it on, I cried till it became wet and cold and clung to my skin, and she had to remove it, dry my tears, and make me blow my nose. Then she kneeled beside me until her face was almost touching mine, and she showed me how easy it was to breathe beneath the mask, so I wouldn't be afraid. She whispered very softly how I was her big girl and Moshe's big sister, and she knew I was brave enough to let her tie another hanky around me—and then it seemed not so scary, though I still didn't like it.

I almost expected the nurse to give me a quick hug or a squeeze the way Mama used to before sending me out to face something on my own. But she walked away and left me standing there. I hurried down the corridor past the broom closet and the laundry and the toilet, and then I slowed my steps as I came to the patients' rooms, because I wanted to peek inside without being obvious. I saw lots of sheets and curtains and pillows and people lying back reading or watching TV or curled up facing the wall or sitting in chairs staring into space. I wondered, Why was Moshe on the other side of the door; was he sicker than all these people? No—I mustn't think like that. "Control your thoughts!" Mama would say. "You're in charge!" But I didn't always feel in charge. He's probably in isolation so he can study, I told myself. Moshe would never tolerate a room where people were watching TV, and nurses and doctors and visitors were coming and going. He needed his solitude.

Excitement and dread surged through me as I approached the door marked ISOLATION—DO NOT ENTER. AUTHORIZED PERSONS ONLY. My brother would always be in a special place where I might come to visit or to pay homage, but never to stay. I believed it was his destiny to be set apart from the rest of us.

I opened the door and entered. Mama looked up, anxiety, weariness, terror streaming from her dark eyes over the mask. In the bed, Moshele was sleeping peacefully beneath a clear plastic tent. His breathing was quiet and unlabored, though he was paler than I'd ever seen him. He was paler than I thought a person could be. When I was in kindergarten, the teacher corrected me when I reached for the white crayon to color the skin of some children in a picture. "White people aren't really white," she said. "They're sort of pink, because they're made of flesh and blood." And she selected a light pink crayon for me. She didn't know Moshe.

"Shhh—don't wake him!" Mama was always giving me directions on how to conduct myself. Didn't she realize that I wasn't a child and that I didn't need perpetual guidance? She offered me her seat, but I declined, and she sank back into it as though her burdens weighed her down.

The room looked bare. There was the bed with the plastic tent and a bottle hanging upside down from a pole with a tube attached to Moshe's arm; there was a metal nightstand, the chair, and a sink with a mirror. But no books, no flowers, no clothes hanging on the hook behind the door; no siddur, no prayer shawl neatly folded on the night table or resting on the blanket where he might finger the fringes even in his sleep. There was nothing in the room to indicate that a unique human personality dwelled there, not a trace, not a suggestion of a Jewish soul. There was no mezuzah—that tiny parchment with Torah excerpts—on the door, no special cup by the sink for making the blessings. These were things I took for granted. We had them at home, and every other home I ever entered also had them. I wouldn't want to live in a house that didn't. I knew Moshe would grieve if he knew these things were missing.

"Shouldn't we buy a mezuzah for the room?" I whispered.

"He'll be coming home in a few days. By next Shabbos, please God, he'll be home already. He doesn't need anything."

"What about his siddur?"

"Better it shouldn't be in a place with all these germs. He doesn't need to read his prayers. He knows them all by heart."

I needed to connect with Moshe. I could picture his soul drifting around the room. Mama and I were concealed behind our masks; the door was closed, the room in "isolation." I felt no relatedness to anyone or anything around me. I wanted to run outside through the doors, down the corridor, through the lobby, and into the sunlight, where pink and brown and yellow flesh-and-blood people lived their lives and talked and laughed and cried and prayed out loud and I would not feel cut off.

It was boring watching Moshe sleep and watching Mama watch him sleep. I was tired of standing still so long; I needed to swing my arms and stretch and draw in fresh air. I was wishing Mama would cry or say something to share her worry so I could comfort her and feel needed. I had had visions of the two of us by Moshe's bedside, our arms around each other, taking turns weeping. I began wondering what it would be like to change places with Moshe; how would it feel for once to be the focus of all their concern? If I were the one who was sick, Moshe probably wouldn't come at all. Mama wouldn't let him; he might catch my germs. And his studies would be considered too important to be interrupted.

Mama broke the silence. "There's chicken from yesterday. You can heat it up for supper. And make yourself some rice or carrots."

"Will Papa be home?" I asked.

"He's meeting me here. He's bringing sandwiches from the store, so don't save any chicken for us. Eat supper and do your homework."

I could picture them side by side on straight-backed chairs in the corridor keeping vigil, ready to jump at Moshe's slightest sigh or flicker of consciousness. They would unwrap their dinner—egg salad with two small cartons of milk. These days, Papa was bringing home less stuff from the store; he was leaving the lox and fancy cheeses alone and concentrating on the cheaper items. He would grasp his sandwich in both hands and down it quickly, darting anxious glances up and down the hallway as though someone might come and snatch it away. He reminded me of a squirrel when he ate. Chomp-chomp-chomp-chomp-chomp! Nourishing his body with the utmost expediency. Eager to demonstrate that the food gave him no pleasure but that he was merely obeying the commandment of his Creator in consuming it. Chomp-chomp-chomp! All gone!

Mama, on the other hand, would show no interest in the sandwich. She would allow it to lie in her lap untouched until, with Papa's urging, she would start picking at it and eat about half.

Then Papa woud remove his little green book of blessings from his jacket pocket, and Mama would take hers out of her bag, and they would say their grace-after-meals quickly and silently, their lips scarcely moving. They didn't need to carry their benchers; none of us did. We knew all the blessings by heart. But it was considered a sign of intellectual arrogance not to use the books each time. I don't think I would have had the courage in the school cafeteria to sit at my place and start murmuring words or moving my lips, unless I had the book in front of me to pretend I was reading.

Mama said, "It's getting late. I want you home before it gets dark. We'll be home about nine thirty."

I said, "Okay," and I buttoned my coat, walked around to her side of the bed, kissed her forehead, and left. It felt so lonely walking away from Mama and away from Moshe, knowing that soon the three of them would be together like a closed circle and I would be left out.

I got off the bus early and walked the remaining five blocks. The air felt clean and sharp, dissipating the stuffy, medicated hospital atmosphere. That was another world, with its own commandments and order, its own ritual and customs. I was glad to leave it behind. It was hard to realize that it existed right alongside my own world and how easily a person could be removed from the normal routine and swallowed up by the hospital. I felt sorry for Moshe. When visiting hours were over, he would be left among strangers in a bare room amid all sorts of tubes and bottles and that awful, cold, antiseptic smell. I was glad I had visited him, for even though he slept, I felt it made a difference that I was there and Mama was there and he was not alone.

As I crossed over to our side of the street, I thought

of Tante Sophie and Rosie. If only I could go to them and be taken in and feel warmed by their concern and their conversation. But things weren't like that anymore. They were their own family, and we belonged to us. We no longer flowed from one to the other; it was all dust between us. If I was to go to them now, it would be as a stranger. We would have nothing to say, no mutual point of touching or sharing. Better I should put them out of my mind, because it only stirred up sadness and a longing I could not satisfy.

# CHAPTER
# 21

Every day, after school, I went to the hospital. Within ten days, Moshe was no longer in isolation. Most of the time, when he was awake, one of his learning partners was with him and I wasn't allowed to intrude. Mama considered it an honor that these Talmud scholars came every day to study with her son; but it made me angry to drag myself to the hospital only to be treated as a second-class citizen. A steady stream of his schoolmates filed into and out of his room. They looked monotonously alike to me—except for one. I thought he must be new at the yeshiva; how long would it take before he looked like all the rest? But for now, he was husky and bare faced, and had a gentle, almost shy smile. He hadn't yet learned the custom of avoiding the glance of women, and so he smiled to me as he left Moshe's room.

"He's all yours. Sorry we kept you waiting."

My face became warm, and I knew I was blushing. "That's all right," I stammered. "I know he needs to study."

"I guess he needs to see his sister, too." He laughed. "I know. I've got four of them." He started to turn toward the elevator but changed his mind. He extended his hand toward me.

"I almost forgot. My name is Jonathan. Jonathan Goldberg. I introduced myself to your mother when I came, but I almost forgot you." He held his hand out, waiting for me to take hold of it. It was the first time a religious boy hadn't shied away from me. His hand was warm and dry and felt very strong, though he took mine only lightly. Then he turned abruptly and hurried down the corridor. My heart was knocking in my chest. I felt giddy. Mama nudged me into the room. "Don't exhaust your brother," she cautioned.

As I entered Moshe's room, I tried to beat back an image that suddenly filled my mind. I saw myself in the bed snuggled close to Jonathan, his lips pressed to mine— just as I'd snuggled with Rosie. It seemed so real, I wondered if Moshe could tell what was on my mind.

Moshe sat like a pale prince propped up by his pillows waiting to receive his callers. But the charcoal rings under each eye and the slightly sunken contour of his cheeks gave him away; he was merely a tired, sick little boy.

"How are you feeling?"

He nodded. "Baruch Ha Shem." Thank God.

Then I didn't know what else to say without sounding like Mama. Casual conversation was never easy with Moshe.

I pulled a chair close to his bed.

"Nothing's new at home," I said. "I miss you."

He smiled almost shyly. "The doctor says I'm improving nicely and maybe I'll be home before next Shabbos. Not this Shabbos, the Shabbos after."

Another whole week—I was disappointed.

Then we both ran out of things to say. I knew it was all right to sit quietly with Moshe—that my presence was enough for him. I hoped no one would barge in and interrupt us.

"Sissa—" Moshe's voice was soft as a breath. "I had a dream, Sissa. Uncle Yitzrok was here. He was sitting right there where you are now."

I didn't think Moshe would ever mention him again.

"And what happened?" I prodded.

"Nothing. He just sat there like you're doing now. He was here, that's all."

I wanted to tell Moshe how I had felt Uncle Yitzrok's presence at his bar mitzvah, but Moshe seemed to know.

"I think sometimes a person can send his spirit to be with someone, even if he can't come himself. Like at my bar mitzvah—"

"I thought you thought he forgot," I said.

Moshe nodded. "He didn't forget." Then he drifted off in thought. "I guess he'll be coming pretty soon, though. To take me to the Holy Land. Remember that night, what he said to Mama and Papa?"

Of course I remembered. "Are you ready?" I asked.

He nodded happily. "I'm ready."

A shadow of fatigue flitted across his face. His study partners had been working him too hard. I rose to go.

"Sissa—" he whispered. "I'm not contagious anymore. You can kiss me if you like." And he bent his head for me to kiss his yarmulke. I wanted to hug him and hold him in my arms, but I was afraid of overwhelming him.

As I neared the door, I remembered Jonathan.

"Who's that friend who left just as I came?" I asked.

"Oh, him. He's new at yeshiva. He wasn't raised Orthodox. But he'll learn."

I hoped not before we had a chance to become friends.

"I think he's cute."

Moshe grimaced. I sensed his revulsion of my physical being. I was sorry I had spoken. He was judging me. Condemning me. I could hear him davening: "Blessed art Thou, O Lord, for not making me a woman."

I turned toward the door. "Shalom," I murmured, and left.

I counted the days till Moshe's return. He would restore Shabbos to us and bring the Shechina back into our midst. I had no doubt that the holiness of the Sabbath had to do with our being together. Friday-night and Saturday meals were the only leisurely ones of the week, the only times we talked and sang and no one was rushing off to go somewhere. But with Moshe missing, there were no songs. Mama cooked the usual foods, but no one had much appetite. The smell of the cholent permeated every crevice of every room long after we had finished eating. The heavy odor of beans and fat meat clung to the curtains, was absorbed into the chairs and the couch, was woven into the fabric of the clothes on my body. I began to wonder how, at the end of Shabbos, the Divine Shechina was able to ascend to heaven, encumbered as she must be from a whole Shabbos of cholent and greasy kugel and golden globules of chicken shmaltz—with no lightness and laughter and song to buoy her flight. I missed the zmirot, their melodies so hauntingly beautiful they could only have been composed in heaven. Instead, I was left with disembodied strands of melody floating through my head, tunes I would try to capture during the week, alone—not so much the musical motifs, but the spirit that was their life. I would hum the songs softly to myself, secretly, so as not to usurp from Shabbos what was rightfully hers. I tried to draw serenity from their gentle rhythms and lilting sweetness, but my efforts felt forced. But soon all that would be set aright again.

All week I planned. I wanted to make his homecoming something special. I bought him a pair of knitted booties, like babies wear, to keep his feet warm in bed. With Moshe soon to come home, I wondered if I would ever get to see Jonathan again. I thought about him a lot during that week. I sat in class caressing my fingers, elaborating on our brief handshake. At night, in bed, I hugged my pillow. I rubbed my cheek against the case, picturing his shy smile and the way he would approach me for a kiss.

I waited for an appropriate moment to speak to Mama about inviting Jonathan for Shabbos. My chance came later in the week when Mama took out the cookie tin. I knew she was going to bake the cinnamon ruggelach for Shabbos, which were Moshe's favorite and which she hadn't made since he went into the hospital. I affected an air of complete detachment, because I didn't want Mama to suspect I was having "impure" thoughts.

"We should make this Shabbos extra special," I suggested.

"Shabbos is always special."

"Yes, but I mean extra special, because Moshe's coming home."

"Moshe's being home will make it extra special."

I wondered how to continue without seeming obvious.

"Don't you think it would be more festive if we had company?" I suggested.

"Your brother's not strong enough for company."

"I don't mean a lot of company . . . maybe just one person . . . maybe his new learning partner. You know . . . what's his face . . ."

Mama lifted her eyes from the dough and gazed into my face. I felt warm all over.

"Jonathan What's-his-face," she said. "You know his name."

"That's right, Jonathan, I forgot," I mumbled. "Maybe we should invite him . . ."

Silence reigned as Mama sprinkled the cinnamon over the moist dough. She dipped her hand into the box of raisins and removed a generous handful, never taking her eyes off me. I watched her out of the corner of my eye, pretending absorption in my self-imposed task of picking out crumbs and lumps of dried scouring powder from between the stove and the work counter with the back of a used matchstick.

She waited until I had finished what I was doing and finally looked her way before she spoke again.

"You know, he could never care for you that way." From the way she emphasized "that," I knew she knew exactly what was on my mind. I felt ashamed to show any further interest in the matter, as though I were standing before her completely exposed—in all my carnal lust. She made no attempt to explain herself. I felt the uncleanness of my body, particularly the unmentionable parts down below.

She took her rolling pin and flattened the dough. I watched her deft fingers tapping and patting the edges to even out the lumps before she cut and shaped each individual pastry. I suddenly felt very tired; I couldn't bear being in the same room with Mama. I needed to withdraw and cover myself. I went to my room, sank into my bed, and drifted into a fitful sleep.

# PART
# 2

# CHAPTER
## 22

The phone was ringing. I heard it even in my sleep. Then it stopped, and the ringing was replaced by Mama's shrill cries.

"Peretz! Come quick! Mach shnell! It's the hospital—"

I jumped out of bed. The light from the foyer hurt my eyes. Mama was in her nightgown. Papa came running.

"He's worse! He's very sick. They want us to come right away."

I pictured Moshele, blue, gasping for breath, the nurses and doctors unable to help. I felt him struggle to rise, as though to begin praying, and I saw the Dark Angel standing in his doorway.

"Yes, yes," Mama spoke into the phone. She scribbled something on a pad of paper. Then she hung up, and Papa held her arm a moment and told her to get dressed while he called a taxi. They didn't notice me standing there. I combed my hair and put on my coat to be ready to leave with them.

"I'll go down and hold the cab when it comes," Papa said. I never saw him move so quickly.

Then there was just Mama and I. I took her coat from the closet and held it for her. She seemed so frail as she reached for the sleeves, I thought she might come apart in my arms. Though I was scarcely seventeen, I felt like the mama, strong and protective. I took her keys and the scrap of paper that she had left by the telephone, and I held her under the arm the whole way down the stairs. Papa was waiting for us in the taxi when we reached the street. No one spoke. Mama's shallow, rapid breathing and the rattle of the motor were the only sounds as we sped through the deserted streets. We sat stiffly and silently in the back. I felt as though I were careening through a nightmare. I wanted to hold Mama and tell her, "Don't worry. It will soon be morning. Then we'll wake up. 'Joy cometh in the morning!' " The line popped into my head from some prayer or psalm, but I couldn't remember which one. Then that line was supplanted by another. "Because he clings to me, I will deliver him. I will save him because he loves me." Suddenly I knew everything would be all right. For I could not think of another living soul who clung to God as my brother did, who left no room in his life for person, activity, or study that did not relate to God, his Redeemer, his Savior. I felt a rush of euphoria as I drew in a deep breath, held it, and let it out slowly. I squeezed Mama's arm and waited for her to glance my way so I could whisper to her, "Because he clings to me, I will deliver him. I will save him because he loves me." I wanted to take away Mama's worry and her pain. But she continued to stare straight ahead, taking no notice of either Papa or me, as though she was concentrating all her energy on making the cab go faster.

"You want the main entrance or the emergency?" The driver broke the silence.

"Main, please." I gave the directions. He pulled up. Papa paid and we got out.

They stood by the curb, his arm draped over her shoulders, without as much as a breath passing between them. You couldn't tell who was supporting whom. In the face of the mammoth hospital complex, Mama and Papa seemed pitifully shrunken. I felt an inexplicable foreboding as I watched them. My fingers were ice; I rummaged for the slip of paper in my coat pocket.

"It says, 'Intensive Care, fourth floor.' " The paper shook in my hand. I walked ahead and held the door for them. A flood of sadness welled up in me; Mama and Papa seemed to have withered and died before my very eyes. I longed to throw myself in Mama's arms and breathe my own life into her, to cry, "Don't leave me—don't leave me!" But I knew I had to act strong.

When we got off the elevator on four, I preceded them to the nurses' desk.

"We're Moshe's family," I said. "We got a call—"

The nurses stopped their conversation. The head nurse stepped forward. She spoke over my head to Mama and Papa, who were behind me.

"I'm so sorry," she said. "Do you want to go to his room?"

She rushed to Mama's side and took her under the

arm; she on one side, Papa on the other, as though it were Mama who was sick. I trailed. When we were outside the door, the nurse asked Papa, "Is it all right if she comes in?" and she nodded in my direction. But I was close behind and followed them.

It was a place of suffocating stillness, as though time had ceased. I felt light-headed, weightless, stripped of thought and the ability to use words. I felt an utter disconnection to everyone and everything in the room. I was without definition in the universe, a free-floating agent. I stared blankly at the bed in its whiteness, surrounded by all kinds of apparatus. I wondered vaguely what I should be looking for. Something seemed to be missing. Something that, if found, would restore my identity. Then I noticed the slender mound beneath the sheet. Suddenly I understood what was missing. The room began to spin. I wanted to pass out, to sink into the ground and let it hold me. I felt sick to my stomach. I turned to run from the room. Papa put his hand on my arm and held me. He made me face him. Then he took hold of his shirt at the throat, staring at me all the while, pinning my attention to him with the force of his gaze, as though he was trying to communicate a strength, a destiny that reached beyond grief. He tore his shirt from his collar to his heart. He nodded to me.

My blouse was worn; the fabric yielded easily. I made a tear right over my heart. I knew we were carrying on an ancient tradition of our people, for "Jacob rent his garment when he saw the blood-drenched robe of his son Joseph." And since then it has been our custom, too. I had learned all this in Hebrew school, but I never understood what it was about. Now I suddenly wanted to destroy more than my garment. I wanted to rip apart the universe. Papa held my wrist and lowered my hand from my bosom when I had torn the prescribed amount. Mama, her dress already ripped, watched silently. Papa took out the palm-size siddur he always carried in his jacket pocket. He recited slowly, waiting for Mama and me to repeat each line. His voice was hollow, lacking in conviction, but it was the commandment to acknowledge Divine Justice.

"*He is God, what He does is right, for all
His ways are just. . . .
He is God, perfect in every deed; who
can say to Him, "What art Thou doing?"
He rules below and above; He causes death
and life, He brings down to the grave and
raises up. . . .
O Thou who art righteous in all Thy ways . . .
and full of mercy, have compassion, have pity
on parents and children. . . ."*

But He didn't. I remember thinking it was all words: "Because he clings to me, I will deliver him. I will save him because he loves . . ." It meant nothing. I didn't think I would ever set foot in a shul again. This was not the kindly, compassionate, and just God of Mercy I had been taught to love and to obey. This was not the God I had pictured as a child, looking down from heaven, listening attentively to all that His Chosen Ones did and said, smiling benignly upon me as I learned to make the various blessings over everything I ate and every ritual washing of my hands, over my lying down to sleep and waking again to life.

I felt tricked. Cheated. God had given me only one brother and now He had taken him away. Why? Moshele was such a good little boy, he loved God so much. He loved me. Why Moshele? Why? Why me? Why not someone who had half a dozen little brothers and sisters? Moshe, Moshele, don't leave me! You're only pretending, aren't you? You always liked to fool us with a straight face—then burst out laughing, and we'd all laugh with you. Remember? Remember, Moshele, my brother, my dear little brother? Say this is just a joke, too. You're lying so still, pretending to be dead. It is a joke, isn't it? Isn't it?

> *"Yisgadal v'yiskadash shmay rabboh*
> *B'olomon dee a'roh chir-usey. . . ."*

> *Extolled and hallowed is the Name of the*
> *Creator. . . .*

We recited the Kaddish by his graveside. It was a clear, sunny morning, a hint of spring, which would soon be with us. As I watched them lower the casket into the grave, I kept feeling they were not burying my brother but rather planting him. In a little while, he would begin to blossom and grow. He would come up every spring, and I would visit with him and know that he would never, ever leave me.

All during the shiva week, men from shul and from the yeshiva came to our house to make a minyan with Papa and recite the Kaddish. Mama and I joined them, though I felt like a hypocrite because I didn't want to praise and extol the Name. All I wanted was someone to sit with me, someone who would understand without talking—because I didn't want to share with anyone the secret bond I had with Moshe. Relatives and neighbors and acquaintances from shul streamed into and out of the house all week, bearing fruit and nuts and sweets to ease the bitterness of mourning. But they all felt like strangers to me—even Tante Sophie and Rosie. From early morning till late at night, people were coming and going, yet an eerie hush prevailed. No one spoke above a whisper. Mama, Papa, and I shuffled about in our slippers in accordance with the traditions of mourning. We seemed to be moving as in a dream. The everyday aspects of our existence had been transformed by death. All the mirrors were draped with sheets in accordance with the Law, to deflect the focus from our transitory and earthly existence. Everyone sat on low chairs or on pillows placed on the floor to be nearer the dead. Papa didn't shave the whole week. The black-and-gray whiskers on his cheeks and the deep, dark rings under his eyes made him look like an aged, homeless beggar. It was frightening how different and unreal everyone seemed. I had the impression that, had I reached out to touch someone, even Mama or Papa, Tante or Rosie, my hand would have passed right through them. Only Moshe seemed real. I could picture him beside me on the sofa pillow overseeing and somberly approving all of our mourning ritual.

With all the coming and going in the house, no one noticed me much, so I was able to sneak off to my room and be alone. Sometimes I tried to understand how things could have changed so quickly—without warning, how my life could be turned topsy-turvy. If I was not Moshe's big sister, who was I? Only a few weeks ago, he was here on the other side of the partition studying. If I kept still even now and held my breath, I could hear him. How could it be that he was gone from me forever? There had to be some mistake. Maybe he had gone away for a little while, but he would return. Any minute now, he might rap on the door, lightly, as he always did. "Sissa? Sissa, can I come in?" For even though we shared the room and it was as much his as mine, he always knocked before he came in, just in case I wasn't dressed.

"It's okay, Moshele. You can come in." I said it aloud now, so it would be real and I could picture it happening.

"Sissa, why are all those people here? Everyone's whispering and crying. What's the matter?"

"It's nothing, Moshele. You mustn't go out there. Stay here, with me."

And I would put my arm around him and make him sit beside me on the bed and hold him close, as I used to long ago when I read him stories or when he cried.

"You mustn't go out there, Moshele. Stay here, with me. Stay here. Stay . . . stay . . . with me. . . ."

Tante Sophie was at our house most of the week, cooking and preparing our meals.

"It's important you eat. You have to go on living," she kept saying to us.

Her manner was more subdued, her voice softer than I'd ever remembered. I was surprised that she knew all the rules of kashrut and Jewish observance; all those restrictions she refused to keep in her own home she followed scrupulously for us. You would never know that she and Mama were scarcely on speaking terms. I wondered if Tante had really changed, or would she revert to her old self as soon as our mourning was over? Would she and Mama continue passing each other on the street with the barest of nods, or would our mutual grief serve to draw our families together again?

Rosie came to visit nearly every day; she helped her mother in the kitchen, or she sat quietly by herself. I kept wishing she would come over and sit by me, although I didn't know what I would say to her. I had nothing to say to anyone. When she left each evening, I felt both disappointed and relieved.

When nighttime came and I finally lay still, a chasm opened up within me. On the one side, I wanted to curse God and curse Mama and Papa and Moshe for taking away everything so that I could never return; and on the other side, I longed to pour my heart out to God my Father, though I doubted He still cared or even listened to me.

I thought about Moshe a whole lot. At first, I tried to pretend that he had gone to the Holy Land with Uncle Yitzrok. I combed the books and magazines at home and in the library for photographs of Jerusalem and Safed, where Uncle would surely take him. I pretended I was with them. We stood at the Western Wall and prayed. We recited the blessing of God, who "revivest the dead," and I felt comforted.

But that didn't work too long, and I began picturing Moshele in the ground, being rained and snowed upon, his lips forever sealed, unable to sing his beloved zmirot or to rejoice in Shabbos. The rabbis say the Afterworld is an eternal Shabbos, but I couldn't picture how that could be with Moshe alone in his grave. One Friday afternoon, I decided to visit him. I wrote a note to my teachers in Mama's hand explaining that I had a severe dental problem and the dentist could see me only on Friday at one. No one questioned it. So, when fifth period ended, I left the building and took the subway to Atlantic Avenue, where I changed for the Long Island Railroad. It didn't seem right to me that Moshe should be sleeping so far from us. If he were closer, I could visit every day, and then, perhaps, I wouldn't miss him so much.

When I got off the train, I stopped at a florist's and bought a small bunch of light-pink roses. They were pale and delicate as Moshe. As I walked the few blocks to the cemetery, I felt a nervous thrill. Would Moshe know I had come and would he, in some mystical way, communicate with me? Would we be able to re-create a sense of Shabbos as it used to be when he was with us? Was I committing a forbidden act in seeking out the dead? At the cemetery office, I asked directions to his grave. There were streets and avenues, as though it were a city of the dead. Row upon row of graves spread out before me. I started down the first lane in search of a small mound without a stone, for it had been only six weeks and the stone would not be placed for eleven months. I passed two small graves where children lay, but I didn't come to Moshe's. The second lane was like the first, and the third as well. Names. Dates. "Beloved . . . husband, father, mother, brother, sister . . ." But no Moshe. I went down the fourth row and the fifth. A truck was parked by an open gravesite. I wondered who would be buried there; perhaps a friend for Moshele. I wondered if Moshele was nearby, hoping I would turn in the right direction and find him. Moshe— Moshele! I began to cry. I wanted my brother. Moshele, where are you? I picked my way between the graves. It was growing late. Mama always expected me home directly from school on Fridays. If only I could find my brother—just to wish him Good Shabbos and give him the flowers! I tried to imagine that I couldn't find him because he was home, preparing for Shabbos, showering and dressing in his navy suit to go to shul with Papa and welcome the Sabbath Queen. And that when I came home he would be there; I would peek around the partition and see him poring over his sacred books. Perhaps he would have a new Shabbos story or a zmira to teach me. I knew it must be after three; I had to start home. I made a mental promise to Moshe to come again.

I was always trying to visit with him, in my mind; remembering how things used to be with us—not just with Moshele and me, but with Uncle Yitzrok and Mama and Cousin Rosie and Tante and Papa. It was as though, if I thought hard and long enough, I might come up with something that would bring my brother back and make everything all right again.

# CHAPTER
## 23

It was late May. Sunlight streamed into the classroom. I watched the specks of dust squiggling and churning in the shafts of light, hazing out the words on the blackboard. Sometimes the voices faded with the words, and I remained only vaguely aware of the rhythms and inflections until I was brought to attention by suddenly hearing my name called. I thought about Moshe. And sometimes I thought about nothing at all. I listened to the birds chirping in the trees outside the windows and to the caretaker's snip-snip-snip as he pruned the hedges, and to the screech of a car as it took a corner on two wheels; I listened to the clacking and grinding of the garbage truck by the curb and the cursing of the workers and an occasional snatch of conversation from passersby on the street. I wondered vaguely what it all meant—what was the purpose of life?—what was the purpose of my life? And when the buzzer sounded, I gathered my books and moved on to the next class.

It was no different at home. I felt that I was drifting or, worse, that I wasn't even there. We'd become like three boarders sharing the same apartment, eating at the same table. No one spoke more than necessary. If ever I had something I wanted to share—a thought or a feeling, a worry or a hope to which I still clung—I felt as though I was intruding upon an ordained silence.

The only school periods I still enjoyed were when I did service for Mrs. Hartman. I liked sitting across from her desk, staring off into space, seeing the familiar book jackets, which were mounted on a background of light-blue construction paper across the paneling over the blackboard. The stacks of magazines and books in "the borrowing corner" and the back bulletin board labeled PAR EXCELLENCE! and lined with stories and book reports all handwritten in blue and black and purple and south-sea ink and liberally adorned with red-penciled "Very good!" "Well put!" "Excellent!" made me feel at home. One of my papers was always among the chosen. It was a place I felt comfortable just being—without the strain of having to explain myself.

One day, as I glanced up from a set of spelling papers, my eyes met Mrs. Hartman's. I felt she'd been looking at me a long while.

"Growing up is very hard, Miriam. I know." Her voice was scarcely more than a whisper. But her "I know" said everything. Suddenly she was sitting beside me while I cried on her shoulder. She kept handing me blue Kleenex from a box on her desk. "I know, I know, it's very hard," she murmured. Her voice was like a brook. She didn't demand that I stop pitying myself, as Mama did, nor did she shove a chore into my hands. She didn't try to take away my feelings. I wanted to hug her and keep her as a friend forever and ever. When I was all cried out and I finally straightened up, I noticed there were tears in her eyes, too. She sent me down the hall to the girls' room to wash my face. When I returned, she was at her own desk, writing something on a piece of paper. She looked up and smiled.

"How would you like an interesting job for the summer?" she asked. "A bookstore in the neighborhood asked the English department to recommend some pupils as sales help. How does that sound to you?"

I'd never had a real job—for money. Even when I used to baby-sit on occasions for a neighbor, Mama wouldn't let me charge like the other girls at school. She insisted I do it as a mitzvah. And baby-sitting jobs weren't even exciting. But now I could be out in the adult world, where grown people would be asking my help to select their books. They would listen to what I had to say. And I'd get to bring home my own money at the end of the week. A job around books, even Moshe would approve! I couldn't wait to tell Mama the good news. She'd be so proud!

I practically ran the whole way home and up the stairs.

Mama was by the sink peeling potatoes.

"Guess what?"

She narrowed her eyes and gazed at me with that expression she used whenever she criticized. I knew right away that I was wrong for barging in on her like this. I felt the inappropriateness of my happiness in her presence.

Suddenly I didn't feel like telling Mama my news. I just wanted to get away from her, to go into my room and slam the door and try to get quiet inside. I knew if I could still myself, after a while I'd begin to feel the presence of my brother. He'd understand about my job. He'd be happy for me.

"Mrs. Hartman offered me a job for the summer in a bookstore."

"That's why you come home from school shouting?"

"I'm sorry." I caught a sharpness in my tone, but it was out and too late to soften it.

"What kind of a bookstore? Do they sell holy books—books for learning—or all that other stuff—sex and violence?"

"I don't know. She didn't say."

"What kind of people come in?"

"I don't know."

"And what will you be doing there, may I ask?"

I hated when Mama questioned me like this. It made me feel as if I were standing trial for a crime. I tried to hide my irritation and my disappointment in her lack of enthusiasm.

"I guess I'll be selling books."

"And they'll pay you for this?"

"Yes!"

Mama considered in silence as she continued peeling the potatoes.

"I suppose it would be good for you," she said. "Where is this store?"

"It's on Fifteenth Avenue."

She nodded. "I'll talk it over with Papa tonight. We'll see what he thinks."

"Talking it over with Papa" was only form. Once Mama decided a matter, that's how it remained. Ever since that day the Partner had paid us that terrible visit, Papa never uttered an opinion or gave a direction or took the initiative in anything. But Mama persisted in "consulting" him and pretending that her decisions were "their decisions." It was a sort of game, which made me feel both sad and angry, because I knew that Mama was doing it to try to make Papa feel good about himself, but I kept wanting Papa to say, "I was wrong to do what I did. I stole from the store and I'm sorry," instead of letting Mama continue to cover up for him.

In the beginning, after the Partner's visit, I kept expecting Papa to make an apology, if not to Mr. Samuel, at least to us, and to let us know that he'd be paying for everything he'd taken over the years. But he never mentioned it, nor did Mama. Then I supposed he'd be looking for a new job, but he stayed on at the store. Apparently, he and Mr. Samuel had reached some sort of truce. The only thing that seemed to change was that Papa withdrew more and more, and he no longer looked us in the eye when he spoke. I sometimes wondered if Papa felt that Moshe's death was God's retribution for his sin.

# CHAPTER
# 24

June 26 was the last day of school. On June 27, I started work. I woke up before daybreak and lay staring into the darkness, trying to relax. I couldn't see the sky, because the partition was still in place. I didn't mind the partition; it helped me imagine Moshe was on the other side.

My mind turned to the bookstore. I wondered what sort of people I might meet there. I had already met the manager, and I had been introduced to some of the other employees. But I knew there would be three more "summer people," students like myself, and I wondered who they would be and whether I might make friends with them. I tried to picture what the customers would be like and whether I would seem like "a mature young woman" rather than a schoolgirl to them. I had my most sophisticated outfit ready for my first day—a navy-blue two-piece dress, which Mama said was "very slenderizing," and a pair of beige leather pumps with little heels. And I had a tube of "peach Melba" lipstick secreted in the zipper compartment of my pocketbook, to be applied when I got a safe distance from the house.

But then I thought of Moshe again. I could feel his disapproval as I made myself up.

I drifted off to sleep, and when I opened my eyes, it was already light and I could hear Papa in the bathroom. We passed each other in the foyer, he all ready for work and I in my robe. I was hoping for a pat on the head like he used to give me and a "mazel tov" for my first day, or maybe a word on how proud he was of me, or a little interest in how I felt this morning and whether I was nervous; I was hoping. But not really expecting. It didn't come.

The air had the delicacy and lightness of a spring morning as I started out. Throughout my body, I felt a sense of freshness and hope—of reawakening. This was my favorite time of day. I could walk at my own pace, contemplating the hours ahead or thinking of nothing at all—not having to dodge bicycles and side-step delivery trucks and open cellars, not even having to wait at corners for the "walk" signal. The streets were mine, the morning was mine! I breathed deeply of my new life. I ran. I paused in front of shop windows to gaze, and pictured myself, slender someday, dressed in the latest fashion. My dreams took flight.

I got to the store an hour before it opened. I peered into the window at all the wonderful books on display—stories of passion and adventure, of mystery—stories of travel, biographies and fiction—best-sellers that people all over the country were reading and discussing—tragedies and comedies that went far beyond the age-old stories of Abraham, Isaac, and Jacob. The romances in Torah were cut-and-dry. "And Isaac brought her into his mother's tent and took Rebekah and she became his wife; and he loved her." I wanted to know how he loved her, what went on in the tent, how did Rebekah feel about her new husband? These books in the window, they would speak of feelings and the nature of love. They would open the doors of life to me. I couldn't wait for the manager to come so I could go inside and hold the books in my hands and leaf through their fine, crisp pages. I decided to try to memorize the titles and authors of all the books in the window. Then, when they opened up, I'd already know a lot and I'd make a good impression.

As I peered into the window, I became aware of a young woman returning my gaze. She had a roundish face, large, dark eyes, shoulder-length brown hair, and she wore peach Melba lipstick. I smiled, she smiled. I stood tall, and so did she. I noted with satisfaction that she looked like a "young woman" rather than a school-girl. She was not obese, as I'd always thought, nor were her pimples as prominent as I'd imagined. In fact, she might almost be considered borderline attractive. There was much of Mama in the shape of her face and her eyes and the expression of her mouth. When the face in the plate-glass window stopped smiling, I could easily imagine the thin lines slanting down from the corners of the mouth. And I could picture those large, dark eyes as mere hollows, the way Mama's had become during the past few months. Perhaps even a few streaks of gray in the hair or sagging bosoms and a big belly from bearing six or seven children, the way so many of the young Orthodox mothers did. They were old housewives though still in their twenties. I would never let that happen to me.

My eye lit on the financial corner. *Investment with a Future. How to Make Your First Million.* I thought with pleasure of the sixty dollars that awaited me at the end of each week. If I was careful, I could save four hundred dollars for the summer after contributing to the house and buying some of those handsome, shiny-covered volumes. I could put the money toward college or my first trip to Israel. I knew that in the Holy Land I would be able to draw closer to Moshe. I knew that my perceptions would be enhanced and that I would understand things I never could before. I would take Mama and Papa with me. Then they would see that, even though I'm a girl and not a Torah scholar, I could bring them naches, joy, and be a source of pleasure to them.

I tried to lose myself in the titles of the books, but Mama's silent gaze kept following me in the plate-glass window, so I decided to go across the street to Dovid's Dairy and sit at the counter and order a cup of coffee. We never had coffee at home, and I knew Mama disapproved; tea was fine, but coffee had the stigma of "the goyische world." It was what "they" were always drinking in their offices and their restaurants—it was a waste of time; it was habit-forming, like cigarettes. I thought it was more sophisticated than tea or milk and more appropriate to my new status of working woman. Besides, I liked the aroma, and when I added a lot of

cream and sugar and drank it with a cinnamon doughnut, it was fine.

The only other restaurant I ever ate in was Shlomo's,
and that was different, because you carried your own
food to the table, and Moshe was always with me, and
besides, I was much younger then. A few months after
Uncle Yitzrok had disappeared, Mama and Papa decided to let Moshe attend an early learning session on
Sundays with some older boys before the regular afternoon classes. It was my job to accompany Moshe the
half mile to school. Mama used to give me money to
buy us both breakfast on the way. We always ate in
Shlomo's Kosher Cafeteria, because we were partial to
their home fries, which were laced with onions and had
a thick, greasy crust from sitting on the grill for hours.
Mama used to admonish me: "Be sure he eats good.
See he orders an egg. Potatoes aren't nourishing enough."
I used to order the potatoes and a big black-and-white
cookie for myself. I liked its intense sweetness and the
fact that the vanilla and chocolate icing were side by
side on one cookie. I used to pretend they stood for
brother and sister. I always broke off a piece with both
flavors and wrapped it in a paper napkin for Moshe to
put in his pocket and save for lunchtime.

The money we spent on breakfast in those days was
Mama's. But this money was mine, as was the choice
to spend part of it on a cup of coffee and a doughnut
and a tip for the waiter, who smiled and said, "Good
morning, young lady!" as he wiped the counter and set
down the menu before me. Everything bustled in this

restaurant. The waiters stacked three or four platters of eggs and toast or pancakes and pastries on their arms at once. Customers rattled newspapers as they ate. Cups clattered in saucers, spoons and knives tinkled, the cash register banged and rang up change for a steady flow of patrons. There was an air of excitement, of coming and going, of productivity. I knew I couldn't do this often if I intended to save my money. But this one day I indulged, and I savored every minute of it.

The clock over the counter read 9:25. My knees were trembling as I stood to leave. All morning, I'd been able to tether my anxiety; my mind was content to muse on all the good things that awaited me. But now that the time was at hand, my fears broke into a gallop. What if I wouldn't be able to learn my duties, if I wasn't able to concentrate? Then they'd think I was stupid; they'd fire me. Mrs. Hartman would be disappointed; Mama would shrug; she wouldn't scold me, but I'd know she was thinking, This is what I'm left with—a daughter who can't do anything right!

# CHAPTER
## 25

Mr. Kresge had just opened up when I got there. He looked at me, and for the second before he smiled, I thought, Maybe he forgot who I am and he'll send me away. "Summer help? We don't need anyone." But then his face broke into a warm grin.

"You're a real early bird, aren't you? That's a good sign. It means you want to work."

I wanted to tell him I'd been there for over an hour, but I felt embarrassed, so I just smiled and said, "Thank you."

"Make yourself at home," he said, waving me inside. "As soon as I get the fan going, you'll be more comfortable. Look around meantime."

The walls and tables were lined with books—all spanking new, with shiny jackets and alluring titles. Signs on the wall indicated: AUTOBIOGRAPHY/BIOGRAPHY, DRAMA, ECONOMICS, FICTION. *Fiction*. That's what I wanted. I longed for the adventure and romance of other lives and other times. I felt suffocated by Borough Park and Mama and Papa and synagogue and school. I wanted to get away. I scanned the array, neatly stacked on shelves from floor to ceiling—all these different stories and characters—each beckoning to me from its own world! It seemed to me a miracle that human beings might be given the ability to create entire worlds, universes, galaxies of characters and imbue them with the semblance of flesh, blood, mind, and soul. Maybe it didn't matter so much that I had no real friends, as long as I could enter into the lives of these fictional characters. Perhaps someday I, too, would become a writer and create my own companions. My heart was racing again, this time with pleasurable excitement. Andersen, Balzac, Barthes, Bellows, Borges, Bowles, Brontë. So many were already familiar to me. I wondered if the Andersen on the top shelf was the same Hans Christian Andersen whose tales I used to lose myself in whenever we had library period in school. My eye had just lit upon *Thomas Mann: Novellas and Stories* when Mr. Kresge came up behind me.

"Miriam, I want you to meet these three young ladies. You'll all be working together. This is Barbara and Phyllis and Susan." They all looked familiar; I had seen them around school.

"Hi," I said. "Is this your first day, too?" I knew it was, and I felt foolish asking a question to which I knew the answer, but I wanted to seem sociable and I couldn't think of anything else to say.

Susan nodded. Phyllis giggled. "She sounds just like you-know-who, doesn't she?"

Then they all giggled.

I wondered if I had said anything silly, if they knew

my question was dumb. I was determined not to be left out of their confidence.

"Who?" I asked. "Who do I sound like?"

"Never mind," said Barbara, and they broke into uncontrollable laughter. I waited for them to stop laughing. I could feel a sort of grin plastered on my face; it felt as if it didn't belong, yet I was anxious to show them that I appreciated their humor and that I could be fun, too, if they would give me a chance.

"Did you see the great selection of books?" I directed my question to the three of them, to whoever would be kind enough to respond.

"Books? What books? I didn't notice any books!" That was Barbara. Her remarks convulsed the other two.

"Did you—did you—see the great books?" Phyllis was imitating me. I wanted to disappear into the book-shelves. I was sorry I had accepted the job. I'd rather be anywhere else. But it wouldn't do to cry, so I decided to ignore them. I wondered what I had done to provoke their response. I felt dumb, as though these girls knew something about me that I didn't. Yet, at the same time, I felt that they were the dumb ones, to be giggling so much when nothing was funny. They were dressed and made up better than I; they wore eye shadow and rouge, and their sleeves were short, whereas mine came nearly to my wrists, in keeping with the rabbinic laws of modesty. But that was still nothing to laugh about. I knew they were Jewish, so they should understand why I dressed as I did. But then Moshe—no one could have been more Jewish than my brother—I understood why he clung to every jot and tittle of the Law, yet I felt alienated by his scrupulosity. I used to feel he was trying to show me up or to let God know he was a better Jew. I wondered if this was how I appeared to Barbara, Susan, and Phyllis. If so, I could always explain: "You see, I have to dress this way. I think it's silly, too. But Mama insists." Or, better yet, maybe I could save up and buy a short-sleeve blouse, because I didn't own one. But I had a sinking feeling that it wouldn't change matters one bit. And I felt ashamed for being ready to turn aside from God's Law in order to court their favor.

When Mrs. Blum came to the back of the store to "put you young ladies to work," I felt relieved. Immersed in work, I would be saved from the pain of my difference. We were given brief instructions on how to help a customer and how to write up a sales slip and find the proper sales tax on a chart; and then Barbara and I were sent to the stockroom to check new arrivals against lists of order forms. I caught Barbara darting a glance of despair toward the others when we were teamed up together. Phyllis shrugged and called after her, "See you later, alligator!"

I was glad to be with only one of them, because I could talk more easily with one person than with three, and there would be no one for her to giggle with. I tried to think of a good opener, something that would sound friendly without being too personal.

"Have you known Phyllis and Sue a long time?" I asked.

"Just Phyllis. We're best friends."

"Oh. That's nice," I said, not knowing what else to say but thinking that it sounded dumb even as the words came out. I wanted to ask her why they were laughing before, but I thought I'd better not. We worked in silence on the lists. It wasn't so bad; I could think my own thoughts. But after a while I wondered if Barbara might not think I was unfriendly, so I tried to start another conversation.

"Do you live around here?"

"Not far."

"I live almost a mile. I counted the blocks," I said. But this aroused no comment, so I let the conversation drop. Silence filled in the spaces between us. We sorted and counted and checked all morning, till our stomachs began to grind out discordant melodies. Then Barbara stood up. "I have to go see what Phyllis and Sue are doing. We're going to lunch together. See you later." And she climbed the narrow stairs to the selling floor.

I had brought a tuna-fish sandwich with me in a brown paper bag, but I'd have gladly brought it home again had they invited me along. I thought it would be very chic to dine in a restaurant and while away the hour in conversation and laughter over coffee and dessert. Only I suspected that I wouldn't really enjoy their conversation; it would probably be no different from the talk at the cafeteria tables in school—mostly who was going out with whom and who broke up with whom and who was meeting whom where and when—and how much weight So-and-so was losing on her diet. I always took an end seat at the table so I wouldn't have to listen to all that. I preferred my own thoughts or a good book. Yet I always felt bad that no one wanted to sit near me. I read furiously, and when I looked up from my reading, and bits and snatches of nearby conversation floated by, or when I was startled into the present by a squeal of laughter or by someone dropping a tray and the student body bursting into applause and shouting, I thought, They're all boring and silly, anyway. And I tried to return to my reading. Lunch period was the time when the sting of feeling left out was sharpest.

Now, as I unwrapped my tuna-fish sandwich, I perused the shelves for a lunchtime companion. There was Mann! I recognized the name because Mrs. Hartman had mentioned him on several occasions. As I reached for the book, I could almost sense her approval. I thumbed through the pages looking for the beginning of a story with an interesting title. Phrases and sentences caught my attention: "It begins by your feeling yourself set apart, in a curious sort of opposition to the nice, regular people . . . You realize that you are alone; and from then on any rapprochement is simply hopeless!"

Yes, I thought, growing excited. That's exactly how it is! "You realize that you are alone. . . ." But if it could be put down on paper to be shared with others, then you weren't really alone. It wasn't truly hopeless.

Mrs. Blum called down to me: "Miriam? The other girls are back from lunch. Have you eaten yet?"

"Yes."

"Good. Why don't you come upstairs for the afternoon? Phyllis and Susan will relieve you." I was reluctant to leave Thomas Mann, but glad for the change of pace. I was glad I would not have to work side by side with the others. It would be fun to meet customers and help them.

I thought that the three girls looked very content and smug and full of dessert and good talk. I tried to tell myself that I didn't need their small talk, after all, and I would stop trying to gain their friendship—though I knew that, should one of them extend as much as a pinky finger to bridge the gap between us, I would seize it.

That first Friday, when I removed a crisp five-dollar bill and a single from my pay envelope and gave it to Mama, I felt as though I was purchasing my freedom. I even sensed that Mama regarded me differently, now that she saw value in what I was doing. The pay gave purpose to my week. It meant another book and something to put away for college.

As the summer progressed, I found myself thinking more and more of my future. I had over two hundred dollars saved for college. Mrs. Hartman would help me choose a school where I could study to become a writer. I would write for the college newspaper and publish my stories in the magazine. Everyone would admire me— but I wouldn't need their admiration anymore, because I would have a whole universe of my own characters— people I created out of my own heart—to keep me company. They would be my friends forever and never abandon me or die. I would give Mama and Papa a lot of money from every book I published. They would see me make good on my own and they would be proud of me.

# CHAPTER
# 26

One Friday afternoon, as Mr. Kresge was giving me my pay envelope, he remarked, "Miriam, you're always off by yourself. Why don't you mix with the other girls?"

His voice was kindly, he wasn't scolding. But I was caught by surprise. My first impulse was to say, "They don't want me." But then I thought, Maybe I don't care for them either. I've got a right to choose who to spend time with.

"I guess they're not my type."

"Type? Type? What's type? You're a young girl. What kind of type could you be?"

What "type" was I? I knew only that I was different. I'd always thought of myself in terms of how I didn't fit. I was too fat, too clumsy, too quiet, too—different. A girl at school once called me "strange"—so I assumed maybe I was strange. But now, talking to Mr. Kresge, who wasn't ridiculing me but, rather, seemed to care—and who wanted to understand—made me try to understand better, too. What "type" was I? I liked to think my own thoughts and to talk about ideas—and feelings—not to gossip and giggle about other people.

So why should I hang out with people who were cruel and teased?

"I don't know what type I am exactly. But I know what I'm not. I know how I don't want to be. And I don't choose to be around the other girls. I'm not criticizing them or anything. I'm just not like them and I don't care to be. . . ."

Mr. Kresge chuckled.

"Well, you're an independent young thing, aren't you?"

I felt myself blush. "Independent" was the last term in the world I thought applied to me. I'd always felt like Mama and Papa's little girl, who needed permission for every step I took. But Mr. Kresge obviously thought I had a mind and a will of my own. I supposed I could be "independent" and still a little "strange" at the same time. Seen in this light, being different wasn't such a bad thing, after all.

After that conversation with Mr. Kresge, I gradually stopped minding when the other girls went giggling to lunch without inviting me. I knew that someday I would make my own friends.

The next morning, Mr. Kresge sent me to work up front.

"I think you can handle it." He smiled. "If you run into any problems or a customer asks you something you don't know, come to me. The new arrivals are on a list by the register and the order catalogue is on the shelf underneath."

I didn't have long to wait for my first customer. He was a boy about Moshe's size, though probably a few years younger. I waited to see where he would go before I approached him. He appeared frightened, as he glanced back first at Mr. Kresge, then at me. I smiled, but he turned his back and meandered around the store, pausing here and there by various shelves, removing a book, glancing back again, then returning it to the shelf. Suddenly I felt I knew what he wanted to do. My chest tightened and my fingers turned cold as I remembered my M & M venture with Moshe so long ago. I must stop this boy before he got himself into trouble, so I walked over to him and whispered, "Can I help you?" My mouth was dry as tissue; I didn't know what sort of response I might get.

He started. "No, ma'am. I'm okay."

"What kind of book are you looking for?"

"Just a book. I wanna read."

"What do you like to read about?"

I kept seeing Moshe in his place. I wanted to hug him—to save him from hurting himself. I was determined—but I wasn't sure how, so I just kept talking to him.

"We have some good books on baseball," I suggested. "Do you like that?"

"It's okay."

"What about the Wild West and the pioneers and Indians?"

He didn't respond.

"Do you like books on how to fix things—you know,

bicycles and things?"

"Indians." It was more a breath than a spoken word. "I like Indians . . . and explorers."

"Come with me. I'll show you where."

I guided him to HISTORY, AMERICAN/YOUNG PEOPLE, unsure what to do next. I'd have to help him get a book he liked without stealing. I was sure he had no money.

After a few minutes of leafing through pages, he decided on a lavishly illustrated volume, *American Indians and Their Customs*. It was a six-dollar book.

"Do you want to buy it?" I asked.

"Yes."

"It's six dollars plus tax. Do you have the money?"

He shook his head. "No."

I thought a moment. Then: "How about if I lend you the money? Then you can pay me back a little bit each week. I'll trust you."

For the first time, he raised his eyes to meet mine. I felt it was worth risking the money, yet I also felt he would make the effort to repay me.

I was filled with elation as I accompanied the boy to the register, removed the money from my purse, and rang up the sale. I wrapped the book especially nicely, with a ribbon and a bow, and handed it to him.

"Thank you, ma'am," he said, and taking the book from me, he left the store without ever looking back.

That "sale" was the happiest one I made all summer.

# CHAPTER
# 27

It was my last week of work before school. I was downstairs checking boxes of new arrivals when Mrs. Blum called to me, "Miriam, you have a visitor!"

I couldn't imagine who would have come to see me. Who knew I was here besides Mama and Papa? I ran up the stairs. A young woman with her back toward me was browsing in the history section. Otherwise, there were only a few customers up front. The woman turned as I approached.

"Rosie!" In my astonishment, I cried out loud enough for everyone to hear. Then I became embarrassed.

"Miriam!" She smiled and clasped my hand in hers. It felt strange to be shaking hands with someone who had once been my closest friend. She must have been feeling the same way, because she drew me close and threw her arms around me. Before I knew it, we were laughing and crying on each other's shoulders.

"I missed you so much," I wailed.

She didn't reply, but patted me gently on my arm.

"I kept thinking how things used to be with us. How close we were—didn't you think about that, too, Rosie?"

Rosie drew back. She reached for a tissue in her bag and offered me one, too.

"That's all in the past. We mustn't dwell on that."

"But don't you ever think about it?"

I wanted desperately to ask her why she had suddenly dropped me as a friend. Was it all because of that Shabbos when we were so close . . . or was it something else? Had she, after all, found me as "strange" and backward as the other kids did? But I didn't want to hear it. Not from Rosie.

We were still crying and holding each other in the middle of the aisle.

"We must look like two crazy ladies." Rosie giggled.

She said "ladies" and not "girls." And then I noticed that she did seem like a woman. She looked around twenty, though I knew she wasn't. Her cheeks were attractively rouged and her lashes lengthened with mascara. She wore a streamlined sleeveless yellow dress that showed up her olive complexion and made her appear taller and thinner than she was. I was wearing a smock over a long-sleeve blouse, and a skirt. I thought she looked beautiful.

"How did you know where to find me?"

"I asked your mother."

"She told you?"

"Of course. Why shouldn't she?"

I heard myself asking stupid questions again, just because I wanted to make conversation and I was afraid to ask her what I really wanted to know. Did she want to make up with me and be friends again?

She continued. "I wanted to talk with you before, when we came for your brother's shiva—"

I felt my throat tighten at the mention of Moshele. Not now, here, in the middle of the store—where everyone can see and hear. It's much too sacred—

I motioned for her to come with me to the stockroom, where we might have some privacy. We sat on two book cartons and Rosie continued: "I didn't know what to say at the time, so I didn't say anything. I guess I must have seemed cold. I promised myself we would talk afterward, but whenever we passed each other in school, either I was with someone or you looked so hurt that I couldn't—"

We both sighed, and then we laughed, but the laughter was strained, unlike those days when we cried and laughed and even breathed together spontaneously, as though we were one person. I was glad Rosie had come to see me, but I did not feel she had come back to me. There was too much missing between us. I felt both angry and sad—because I longed to fill up the void that had grown between us and to recapture our past together, though I knew it could never be done.

"I couldn't put off seeing you any longer if I wanted to say good-bye," Rosie said.

"Good-bye? But where are you going?"

She laughed. "Don't look so sad. It's not forever. I'm going to college."

"But where? Won't you still live at home?"

"I don't want to live at home. That's why I applied where I did. It's in upstate New York. I'll live in a dorm. But I'll come home for Thanksgiving and the Christmas holidays and—"

"Christmas?"

"You see, there you go again! Don't look so horrified. In the outside world, they call it Christmas holidays, not Hanukkah. What's the big deal?"

I felt she was scolding me.

"The way you looked just now when I said Christmas—you know what it reminded me of?"

I shook my head.

"Remember that Saturday when you passed me on line outside the movie? The expression on your face—I felt you were saying, 'Oh, Rosie, how can you be such a sinner?' I felt you were judging me. Like you felt you were so precious and holy. It made me mad."

I grew warm all over. I knew the "look" she meant. I had often observed it in Moshe, and those were the times I wanted to bring him down. I called it his "holier-than-thou" look, or sometimes his "pious Peter" look. But I never imagined that I, too, had that expression— and that other people saw me that way.

"I wasn't judging you," I whispered. "I missed you, that's all." But I thought, Maybe I was judging you, just a little. Not as bad as Mama used to judge your mama, though, because I would have forgiven you in an instant.

Rosie said, "That's all right. It doesn't matter now. I guess I was no angel."

I wondered what she meant, but she didn't explain. We both lapsed into our own thoughts. Then she con-

181

tinued. "I can't come home weekends. It's too far. But maybe you could come visit me? Lots of girls live near school, so they go home weekends and then there's room in the dorm for guests."

I would love to visit Rosie—and to see what an out-of-town college was like! But I knew Mama would never let me spend Shabbos away from home among non-observers.

"I don't think I could. Mama wouldn't like—"

"Oh, that's right." She drew a deep sigh as she exclaimed, "Shabbos!" I couldn't tell whether she was sympathizing with our observance or ridiculing it. She slipped back into her thoughts for a moment. And then she broached what had always been an unapproachable subject—Uncle Yitzrok.

"I know Papa believed in all that stuff—the Shechina and all that. So what he did was all right—for him. He went to search for it, to live his life for it. I'm not blaming him. In fact, I respect him for it. But I don't believe in that stuff. I think it's a lot of nonsense. So why should I keep Shabbos? It would be hypocritical. There are other things in my life. Other values—"

"Like what?" I couldn't imagine what kinds of values any Jew could entertain that were not based in Torah.

"Like equality for women!" The words flew out of her mouth. I could feel her rage. "I'm not going to live my life in a society that relegates women to a role of passivity. Kitchen, *kinder,* and the back of the shul! And I'm not going to include myself in any group that discourages free thought."

"What group is that?"

"I've been doing a lot of reading. History, sociology, politics—that sort of thing. I'm going to major in political science. The big thing I've learned—you know what that is?"

She didn't pause for me to respond.

"That any group, if it's going to survive, has to suppress the freedom and individuality of its members. Because once people start thinking for themselves and acting on their thoughts—then the group pulls apart. And that's exactly how it is in Orthodoxy. Tradition! You're supposed to follow it because your mother followed it and her mother—just because Jews for thousands of years did something a certain way, you're supposed to do it that way, too, without questioning—without thinking it through for yourself, just following orders. They brainwash you. But God gave me a brain, and I intend to use it!"

She sounded as if she wanted to rip apart everything she'd been taught, at least by her papa, and everything we had shared. I wondered whether she saw me as another stalwart, brainwashed guardian of tradition.

Her anger frightened me. I thought, She has nothing to lose by taking a strong stand! She never experienced the Shechina for herself. She never thrilled to the delights of Shabbos. I felt sad to realize that all those Shabbosim we spent together were nothing more to her than afternoons of song and play. I had always imagined that we were sharing something wonderful and mystical—and that the Shechina smiled upon our friendship

183

and blessed it because we came together each week to rejoice in Shabbos. Perhaps all the while she was sitting at our table, she was thinking what superstitious, old-fashioned fools we were—as Tante had said to Mama. And that when I thought I knew Rosie best, I knew her least. Or maybe we really were as close then as I'd imagined, but that she'd changed since. I wondered what part Uncle Yitzrok had played in all this.

"Do you ever hear from your papa?" I asked.

Her lips twitched; for a moment, I thought she might start to cry; but then she smiled bitterly. Her voice was heavy with scorn.

"Papa is a perfect example. He was so enamored of what the rabbis told him, he was such a stickler for the Law—he believed so wholeheartedly in the ethic of male superiority that he never questioned anything—not even himself. When he wanted to leave, he just left, that's all. Mama and I didn't count, we were only females, after all. A woman's purpose is to bear a man's babies and keep his house and cook his food—oh yes, and scrub and wash and clean for his Shabbos."

I thought of all the evenings he spent in our house, weaving magnificent stories, tilting back in his chair with his lids drawn, drinking schnapps. I thought of his hand on Mama's arm and the pleading expression in his eyes when he said, "Please! Sarah—please! You know what I need—please!" There was so much that Rosie didn't know about her papa. She thought he left because she and her mother were not observant Jews, because they did not "follow orders." "Orders"—"commandments"—they were all the same to Rosie. She made Orthodox Judaism seem like some sort of Fascist state. All her books on sociology and politics were unable to draw a distinction, and she had never learned the difference at home. Yet I agreed with so much of what she said. I didn't want to listen to her anymore. I was afraid she would poison my memory of Uncle Yitzrok and punch holes in my perception of how things were between us in those early years. I was relieved when she said, "I have to go now. I still have more shopping to do before I leave."

"When are you leaving?"

"Wednesday. But I'll be back, like I said. I'll see you Thanksgiving."

I thought, What about our holidays? Rosh Hashanah, Simchat Torah? Why not then? You accept Thanksgiving and Christmas as law without questioning it. You dress according to their unwritten law. Why is that better than the Law you were born into? You're as much a stickler for their customs as we are for ours. Yet I admired her outspokenness—her freedom of spirit to leave home and make a life for herself among people of her own choosing. I'd been thinking about college for a long time, but I never would have dared living away from home, immersing myself in a goyische world. I doubted that I would be able to take the Shechina and my brother with me into diaspora, and I didn't want to leave them behind. Yet I admired Rosie's ability to free herself of the limitations of our closed society. She looked lovely in her sleeveless yellow dress and her rouged cheeks. She looked as though she belonged out there. I felt as though I had shtetl scrawled all over me.

After Rosie left, my head was spinning. I couldn't concentrate on anything. I kept wondering why she had come. I wanted to believe it was out of love and a desire to renew our friendship, but I kept feeling she had come to make a point about religion, to show me how far beyond it she had advanced. I knew she would gladly welcome me into her way of life, but what if styles changed and she changed along with them? She would abandon me again. She would say I was "old-fashioned" and "behind the times." But wasn't it she who was "fashioned," because fashions keep changing? So what if I was connected to the past?—I was also linked to the future. It was the same thing. But she was linked to nothing—a "free spirit"—free to be buffeted around by the changing times. But then, what did I see as lying in store for me? Kitchen, *kinder,* and the back of the shul? Being told that high school is enough, that I don't need to learn more or know more because I'm a woman?

I wished I were a child again, with Mama and Papa teaching me to make my blessings and God smiling on everything I did. It was so simple then.

# CHAPTER
# 28

I left work early and went directly to the Long Island Railroad. I made my way to the cemetery and then to his grave, this time with no difficulty, as though I were being led. I didn't know what it was I wanted to tell Moshe, I just needed to be with him. Uncle Yitzrok used to say that when a Jew dies, as soon as he is buried, his body makes its way through the earth to the Holy Land, there to rest in peace. It didn't bother me that Moshe was in Eretz Yisroel and not here—just as I knew his soul was with God and not on earth. I still felt his presence. I sat on the grass at the foot of his grave and rested my hand on the mound, just as I used to slip my hand through the bars of his crib, seeking my own tranquillity in his gentle slumber.

I wanted him to know that I still loved him, that I would always love him, even though I could not follow in his path. I could no longer accept on blind faith all those commandments and traditions I used to accept when I was a child. I could feel Moshe's sadness for me, as though he were mourning my loss of something beautiful and profound.

I wanted him to know that I couldn't follow Rosie's

way, either. Life without the Holy One, a single day without blessing His Name when I lay down to sleep and when I woke again to life, would be unthinkable. But I would have to find my own way. I didn't know how I would do this. I didn't think I could do it in Borough Park. I needed to get away, to establish my own ties, to make my own life. I could hear Uncle Yitzrok exclaiming, "If a person can't find the Shechina in his own home, he has to seek elsewhere!" And I could also hear him gently remonstrating with Moshe as I stood in the doorway listening: "If a person cannot find the Shechina right there where he is, maybe he isn't seeking hard enough." And I didn't know which was true.

I wanted Moshele to give me the answer. But the silence was palpable.